Stuart Yarnold

Troubleshooting your PC

in
easy steps

Second Edition

In easy steps is an imprint of In Easy Steps Limited
4 Chapel Court · 42 Holly Walk · Leamington Spa
Warwickshire · United Kingdom · CV32 4YS
www.ineasysteps.com

Second Edition

Notice of Liability
Every effort has been made to ensure that this book contains accurate
and current information. However, In Easy Steps Limited and the
author shall not be liable for any loss or damage suffered by readers
as a result of any information contained herein.

Trademarks
Microsoft® and Windows® are registered trademarks of Microsoft
Corporation. All other trademarks are acknowledged as belonging to
their respective companies.

In Easy Steps Limited supports The Forest Stewardship Council (FSC),
the leading international forest certification organisation. All our titles
that are printed on Greenpeace approved FSC certified paper carry the
FSC logo.

MIX
Paper from
responsible sources
FSC® C020837

Printed and bound in the United Kingdom

ISBN 978-1-84078-433-6

Contents

13 Miscellaneous 175

Index 187

1 Before You Start

Introduction

All computer faults fall into one of two categories – hardware faults and software faults. Establishing which is a key part of successful troubleshooting as, by doing so, you immediately eliminate a whole host of issues that you may otherwise have investigated.

Occasionally, it will be quite obvious where the problem lies; for example, when your power supply unit announces its demise with a loud bang and puff of smoke. Usually though, the solution won't be so clear-cut; indeed you may even find yourself in a situation where the problem could be both hardware and software related. A classic example of this is when the PC's boot procedure starts but then stops before the operating system has loaded. This can be caused by a faulty motherboard, CPU, memory, hard drive or video system. It can also be caused by a damaged or misconfigured operating system. But which? Where do you start?

That's where this book comes in. While it doesn't cover all possible faults (there are a million and one things that can go wrong with a computer), it does explain the more commonly experienced problems and how to resolve them.

In the majority of cases, these problems are software related and, of these, most will be an issue with the operating system. It follows therefore, that the majority of the fault finding procedures and tips in the book concern the operating system.

While many of these software faults are common to all operating systems, some are not and, as we can't cover all the various operating systems, the book focuses on the one most commonly used – Windows 7. You'll learn how to troubleshoot Windows 7 itself, and how to use it to troubleshoot other parts of the system, including hardware.

However, if you are using a different operating system, don't let this put you off. Windows Vista is very similar to Windows 7 and so virtually everything in the book is relevant to this operating system as well.

With regard to hardware, troubleshooting techniques are much the same for all operating systems and so the book will be useful whatever your setup.

Don't forget

The screenshots used in this book are taken from Windows 7. The troubleshooting procedures and tips also relate to this operating system.

Common Causes of PC Faults

Before you start pulling your PC to bits, you should be aware that most faults are user-induced. So it's quite likely that the problem is due to something that you have recently done on the PC.

Therefore, the first thing to do is to think back to what you were doing immediately prior to the fault manifesting itself. If you can identify something specific then very often simply "undoing" it will resolve the problem.

The following are the most common causes of computer faults:

Downloading from the Internet

There are hundreds of thousands of known viruses and more are being developed all the time – the vast majority being spread via the Internet. Problems caused by viruses range from minor nuisances to full scale disasters. On a related note, there is also the issue of malware. Some of these programs, or a multitude of them, can literally bring a computer to its knees.

So if your PC starts playing up after an Internet session, particularly if you've downloaded something, there is a good chance it has attracted an unwelcome visitor. Obtain up-to-date virus and malware removal programs and scan your system with them.

Installing a Hardware Device

Installing and configuring hardware with recent operating systems such as Windows 7 is usually very straightforward.

If it's a modern device it will almost certainly use the USB interface; all you have to do is install the driver and then connect the device to the PC when prompted to – Windows does the rest.

However, if you have an old PC, are using an old operating system, or the device being installed is old, then you are quite likely to run into problems. These are usually incompatibility issues between the device and the operating system and can often be resolved by simply updating the device's driver.

Getting the connections wrong is another common source of problems. For example, connecting a speaker system to the wrong output jacks. As a general rule, simply undoing everything you've done, reading the instructions carefully, and then starting again will, more often than not, resolve the issue.

...cont'd

Beware

Be very wary of installing Shareware and Freeware programs downloaded from the Internet. They often contain an unwelcome attachment.

Hot tip

When uninstalling a program, you may see a message stating that files about to be deleted might be required by other applications and offering you a choice as to whether to keep them or not. Always choose to keep these files just in case they are needed.

Don't forget

Changing a computer's settings without fully understanding the possible consequences is a major cause of so-called faults.

Installing New Software

Although relatively rare, there are programs that are not compatible with the operating system being used. Uninstall the program and see if the issue is resolved. If not, a compatibility update may be available from the manufacturer's website.

You should also be aware that malware is often attached to legitimate programs available on the Internet. When the program is installed so is the malware (without your knowledge). The problem here is that uninstalling the program will not uninstall the malware. You will also have to run a malware removal program to get rid of it.

Uninstalling Software

Often we install a program to try it out and then, having decided we don't want it, uninstall it. With most programs there is no problem. However, there are some that simply refuse to go quietly. The usual problem is that these programs "borrow" files already on the system and then, when they are uninstalled, take these files with them. Any other programs on the PC that need the files will then not run correctly, if at all.

Running a Program

Sometimes, simply running a program will cause problems. This might happen because it has become corrupted or is conflicting with something else on the system.

Most commonly in this situation the PC will become unstable or slow down. Close the program with the Task Manager (see page 182), reboot and then run the program again. In many cases this will resolve the issue. If not, reinstall the program.

Changing Your PC's Settings

Operating systems (Windows in particular) offer numerous customizing options that enable the user to make many changes to the default settings. While most of these relate to a specific function or application, and so do not have a system-wide effect; there are some that do – registry and BIOS settings in particular.

If you do experience problems after changing a setting, undo the change to resolve the issue. If you can't remember what you did, use System Restore (see page 38) to undo the change.

Shutting Down Your PC Incorrectly

There is a right way and a wrong way to shut down or restart your computer. The right way is to press the operating system's Restart or Shut down button.

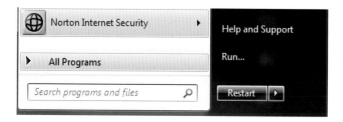

The wrong way is to hit the reset or power off button on the system case front panel . This can corrupt any program that might be running, including Windows itself. In the case of Windows, it may result in you not being able to get the computer running on restart.

Usually, though, the effects are minor and can be repaired by restarting and then exiting in the proper manner, and running Chkdsk (see page 50).

Maintenance

If you have been cleaning the system case, inside or out, or a peripheral such as your printer, it's quite possible that you have inadvertently loosened or even disconnected something. Retrace your steps, making sure all boards and cables are firmly seated in their sockets.

Maintenance in Windows can also cause problems; for example, you may have been using a tuneup utility such as a registry cleaner. Some of these programs can cause more problems than they solve. In this type of situation, System Restore will get you out of trouble.

Upgrading

Replacing or adding parts to the system can cause all sorts of problems. Connections may be incorrect or not made at all, the device may be incompatible with the operating system or a program on it, or the device may be incorrectly configured. The solution is to uninstall the device's driver, remove the device from the system and then start again.

Hot tip

Many problems can be resolved by the simple expedient of rebooting or switching off and then on again. These actions will clear the memory and often reset misconfigured settings.

11

Read the Instructions

Another frequent cause of problems, particularly when installing a new hardware device, is neglecting to read the installation instructions. Some devices are very simple to install but others require a bit more attention.

Some require changes to be made to the default settings in the BIOS. For example, if you install a sound card it will be necessary to disable the sound system integrated in the motherboard. If you don't the system will use the integrated sound system by default.

Video cards also require changes in the BIOS. In this case, the interface the card uses must be specified. For example, if it is a PCI-Express video card, PCI-Express x16 must be selected in the BIOS.

It's not uncommon for some devices or programs to be sold with known bugs that can cause incompatibility issues with other hardware or software on the system.

Furthermore, very often these will not be documented in the installation manual but rather in a file on the installation disk entitled "README" or similar. Taking a few minutes to read these instructions can save a lot of head-scratching and frustration.

Don't forget

Some applications, video card drivers in particular, can be the cause of incompatibility issues with your system. These are often documented in a "Readme" or "Help file" on the installation disk. Make a point of reading these files as doing so can save a lot of time.

All you have to do is right-click the CD/DVD icon in My Computer and then click Open. This will reveal the contents of the disk. If you see a "README" file, as shown in the screenshot above, take the time to read it.

Isolating the Fault

Sometimes you will have absolutely no clues as to what is causing the problem. It will be a head-scratcher knowing even where to begin. In situations like this you need to think logically and eliminate as many possibilities as you can.

First, establish whether the problem is a hardware or a software fault. If there are no clues as to this either, reboot the PC into Windows troubleshooting mode (known as Safe Mode – see page 37) and if the fault has now disappeared, you almost certainly have a hardware issue. If it hasn't, it will be software-related.

Once this has been established, you will have much fewer things to consider.

If Safe Mode indicates a hardware fault, the simplest method of pinpointing the offending device is to, one by one, disconnect as many of them from the system as you can, rebooting each time until the faulty one has been isolated.

You then need to establish whether the fault lies with the device itself or with its connections. The latter is the most likely so check this out first. If the issue is still unresolved, the device is faulty and will need to be replaced.

Software faults are often much more difficult to isolate as very often there can be more than one cause. Windows provides a number of useful troubleshooting and information utilities with which most faults can be rectified. However, using them does require more knowledge than the average PC user is likely to have. A typical example is the System Configuration utility, which can be used to isolate software issues on a trial-and-error basis.

Serious faults with Windows 7 are, strangely enough, often not too difficult to resolve. They can usually be fixed with the aid of several troubleshooting and repair utilities located on the installation disk.

For example, if Windows refuses to start, one of these utilities, Startup Repair, will check the files used to start Windows and if it finds any that are missing or corrupt, will replace them from the original files on the disk.

Don't forget

The first step is to establish that the fault is either hardware- or software-related. This narrows down the number of possible causes considerably.

Hardware Substitution

In Chapter Two, we'll see how to troubleshoot faulty system hardware, e.g. memory and video, with a diagnostic program that produces a series of coded beeps. For example: faulty memory is indicated by continuous beeping, while a faulty video system is indicated by eight beeps.

However, it must be said that this method can sometimes be rather ambiguous. A typical example is when a motherboard is flagged as being faulty when, in fact, it is the CPU or memory (both located on the motherboard) that is the cause of the issue.

If you didn't know better (and most users don't), you would buy a new motherboard and then take the CPU and memory out of the old board and install them in the new one. This would be a waste of time and money.

In the above scenario, what you should do is first check the memory by substituting it with one of the same type that you know is good. Then do the same with the CPU. This establishes clearly where the fault lies – CPU, memory or motherboard.

The same principle applies to other system hardware, such as the video card and the monitor. These parts are expensive and you don't want to be shelling out your hard-earned cash unnecessarily – you need to be certain that the part in question is faulty before going out and buying a new one.

If you don't have a replacement at hand (how many people keep spare CPUs, motherboards, etc, lying around?) try making a few phone calls to friends and family. As many people do upgrade their computers and keep the original parts for just this sort of purpose, you may well unearth what you are looking for. Another possible source is a local computer repair shop – these will have no end of used parts just lying around. Talk to the guy nicely and he might just give it to you!

With this scenario in mind, should you ever decide to upgrade a working device to improve the capabilities of your PC, instead of throwing it away, keep it; you never know when it might come in handy.

Anatomy of a Computer

If you want to be able to deal with hardware problems, it will help
enormously to have some knowledge of your PC's components
and where to find them.

Inside the Computer

Power supply unit   Memory   Case fan   CD/DVD drive

Motherboard   Expansion card   Hard drive   Floppy drive (hidden)

...cont'd

At the Back of the Computer

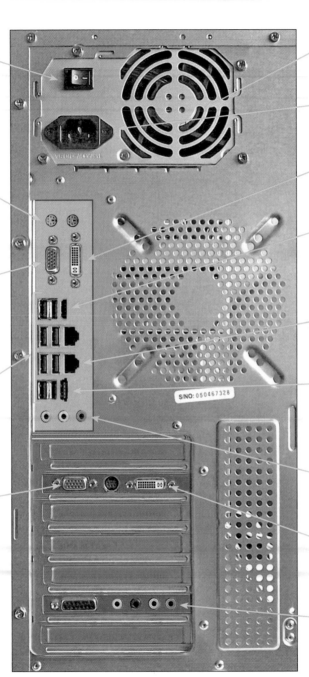

Power supply unit on/off switch

PS/2 ports. The green one is for the mouse, the purple for the keyboard

VGA socket. Used to connect monitors to the PC

USB ports. USB is the standard type of connection

Video card VGA output to the monitor

Power supply unit fan air intake

Power cord socket

DVI socket. Used to connect LCD monitors

HDMI socket. Used to connect external video equipment

LAN (local area network) socket

eSATA socket. Used to connect external hard drives

Motherboard audio sockets.

Video card DVI output to the monitor

Sound card audio sockets

Motherboard

Ports | CPU power | CPU socket | Chipset | Memory slots | Motherboard power socket

BIOS chip | PCI Express x16 video card socket | PCI Express x1 socket | PCI socket | ATA drive socket | SATA drive sockets

...cont'd

The Drive Cage

Located at the front of the system case, the drive cage is where all the drives in your system are installed.

CD/DVD drive

Floppy drive

Hard drive

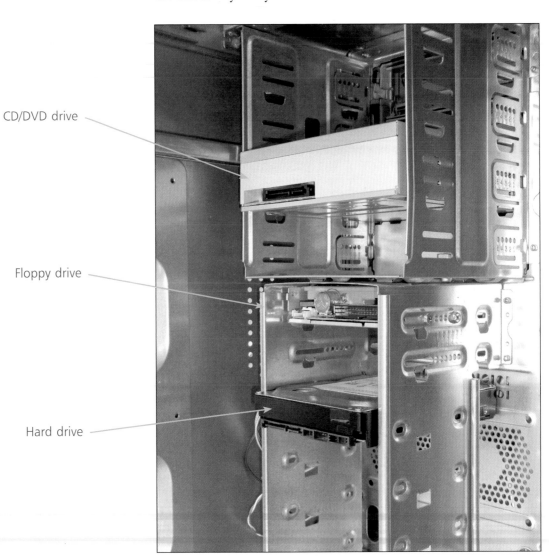

Note that modern computers are no longer supplied with Floppy drives. However, if your PC is several years old it will probably have one. If so, it will be in the location shown above.

Your Computer's Parts

Motherboard

The motherboard is the large circuit board that you will find screwed to the right-hand side panel of the system case.

This board is the heart of the computer and every component, including all the peripheral devices, is connected to it. It provides sockets for the CPU, the memory, expansion cards such as video and sound cards, and the drive units. It also provides ports of various types (located at the top-left of the board) for the connection of peripheral devices such as external drives and printers.

Of all the hardware devices in a PC, the motherboard is the most difficult to replace. This is because all the other devices have to be disconnected from it, the CPU, memory and any expansion cards have to be installed in it and, very often, devices such as the power supply unit have to removed completely in order to get access to it.

That said, as long as you make a note of what goes where, or take some pictures, it is actually a relatively straightforward task to replace one of these boards.

Hot tip

When a motherboard is replaced, some settings in the BIOS will need to be changed depending on what type of hardware is in your system.

Central Processing Unit (CPU)

The CPU is the brains of the computer as it carries out all the calculations, processes instructions, and manages the flow of information through the system.

It is usually located at the top-left of the motherboard and is hidden by a heatsink/fan assembly that prevents it from overheating.

As with all other parts in the PC, the CPU is easy enough to replace. However, you do need to know what you are doing, so should you decide to attempt it be sure to read up on the procedure first. ("Building a PC in easy steps" by this author gives full instructions.)

Random Access Memory (RAM)

A computer's memory consists of a circuit board (known as a module) on which are a number of memory chips and associated circuitry. Its function is to provide an electronic holding place for instructions and data that the computer's CPU can access quickly.

When a computer is running, essential parts of the operating system are loaded into the memory, as are any programs in use. Some hardware devices, such as sound and video systems, also use the memory.

Memory modules are very easy to replace as they simply plug into a socket on the motherboard.

Hard Drive

The hard drive is where a user's data is stored. These are electro-mechanical devices that contain a number of ceramic or glass storage discs coated with a magnetic layer. In a procedure known as formatting, the operating system writes a file system on to the magnetic layer, which enables the drive to locate data when requested to do so.

Replacing a hard drive is a very simple operation that requires four screws to secure it in place. Then it is connected to the motherboard by an interface cable. It also needs a power connection, which comes from the power supply unit.

It then has to be partitioned and formatted by Windows after which it will be ready for use.

Video System

The video system is responsible for producing the picture that you see on the monitor – without it the monitor would be blank. Two types of video system are used in PCs: a video card that plugs into the motherboard (shown right) and an integrated video system that is built in to the motherboard.

Most PCs use integrated video as this is the cheapest option for the manufacturers and, for most purposes, it is perfectly adequate. However, integrated video is not as good as a video card, which is essential for some applications, e.g. games and business applications such as Computer Aided Design (CAD).

A video card is also much easier to replace as all you have to do is plug it into the motherboard and then connect the monitor to it. To replace an integrated system, you will have to replace the motherboard as it is part and parcel of the board.

Sound System

Sound systems are much the same as video systems in that they come in two types – integrated sound and sound cards. The pros and cons of both types are the much the same as for the two types of video system.

CD/DVD Drive

This device serves two purposes:

1) It provides a means of importing data to the PC, e.g. installing a program from a CD or DVD

2) In the case of writable models, it provides the user with removable data storage options, i.e. you can write data to a disc and store it in a separate place. This provides a good way of backing up important data

The difference between CDs and DVDs is essentially the storage capacity of the disc – 700 MB with a CD and 4.5 GB with a standard DVD, and the speed at which data is written and read.

Beware

Should you ever replace a video card, make sure it is compatible with the motherboard. Modern video cards use the PCI-Express interface while older ones use the AGP interface.

Hot tip

CD/DVD drives have an internal lens that reads the data on the disc. Over time, this lens can become obscured by grime and, as a result, may have trouble reading discs. Typical symptoms of this include the drive taking a long time to read a disc or even the PC locking up.

Before you replace the drive, try cleaning the lens with a lens cleaning disc. They don't always work but it's worth a try.

This device is usually located at the top of the drive cage and is very easy to replace. As with the hard drive, there are four securing screws and two connections – power and data. However, there is no need for partitioning and formatting – connect it and it's ready for use.

Power Supply Unit (PSU)

Computers use direct current (DC) so they need a device to convert the alternating current (AC) that comes in from the mains supply – this function is provided by the power supply unit. These devices also provide different levels of DC output, e.g. 12V, 5V, -5V, and -12V to suit the requirements of the various components in the PC.

Usually located at the top-rear of the system case, PSUs are the most likely of all a PC's components to give trouble. The main problem is that they all eventually fail (being a highly stressed component, this is inevitable).

With a good quality model, this is not too much of an issue – it just stops working, the PC goes dead and the user fits a new one. However, low quality units will literally burn out with a loud bang and, in the process, send a surge of current through the system that can damage other components, the memory in particular.

Another problem with low quality PSUs is that the current they supply tends to fluctuate. This means that the PC is sometimes not getting enough and at other times it is getting too much. If these variations in current exceed the tolerances to which the PC's components are built, it behaves erratically. This results in an unstable PC, and often premature failure.

2 Hardware

Chapter Two focuses on what to do if you can't get your computer to bootup. We look at all the hardware devices that can cause this problem, how to identify which device is causing the issue and how to resolve it.

Bootup Fails to Start

When a computer fails to boot up, i.e. to start, it can happen in one of two ways:

1) The boot procedure fails to start at all – all you see is a blank screen

2) The boot procedure starts but fails to complete

In the first scenario, the problem will be an essential hardware device that is not functioning. However, it doesn't necessarily mean that the device in question is faulty – it could simply be a bad connection somewhere.

In the second scenario, the problem could be either hardware failure (see pages 31–34) or a software issue (see Chapter Three).

Whichever it is, the first step is to identify which of the PC's devices has failed. To help users do this, all computers have a diagnostic utility that examines essential hardware when the computer is started and alerts the user when it finds a device that is not working.

It does this in one of two ways: a series of coded beeps, known as beep codes (see page 30) or a text error message on the screen – see bottom margin note.

The diagnostic utility is built in to the system's BIOS, which is a small chip located on the motherboard that handles all the routines necessary to start the computer. These include identification and testing of the computer's hardware, and loading of the operating system.

Knowing what these routines are and the order in which they are carried out can be useful when trying to isolate a faulty hardware device – see page 30.

To begin with, we'll see what to do when faced with a computer on which the boot procedure fails to start. In this situation, the screen will be blank when the PC is switched on. If you hear a beep code, use the table on page 30 to see what device it relates to. Whichever device it is, this will be your starting point.

However, if you don't hear a beep code, or don't understand its meaning, then troubleshoot your hardware devices in the following order.

Hot tip

If the symptoms indicate hardware failure, don't despair. The problem could well be no more than a loose connection.

Don't forget

If a faulty part is found before the video system has initialized, you will hear beep codes. If it comes after, you will see a text error message.

24

The Power Supply

The first thing to establish is whether you have power available to your PC. This principle applies to any electronic or electrical device. For computers it is easily established by observation.

Check the following:

- Are the LEDs (lights) on the system case lit?

- Are the power supply unit and motherboard fans running? Check by holding your ear to the side of the system case; if either of the fans is running, you'll hear it

- Do you see any lights on your keyboard?

- Does the computer make a beeping sound when it is switched on?

If the answer to any of these questions is yes, then the system's power supply is operational. This narrows the problem to one of four devices – the monitor, the motherboard, the memory or the video system – go to page 26.

If the answer is no, then check the following:

- Is there power at the wall socket? Plug another appliance into it; if that works then the socket is OK

- Are you using a surge suppressor, cable extension or some similar device? If so, try removing or bypassing it and see if that solves the problem

- Check the fuse in the plug, and that the connections inside the plug are good

- Next, check the PC's power cable. Try substituting it with the cable from another piece of equipment, such as an electric kettle – these are often the same type

- Most PSUs have an on/off switch at the top-rear of the case. Check that this isn't in the off position

If none of these is causing the problem then the PC's power supply unit is defective and will need replacing.

Hot tip

The first thing to check when your PC appears to be dead is the power supply. Don't forget to check the external (mains) power supply as well.

Don't forget

The easiest way to establish that the power supply unit is operational is to check that the fans are running and that the keyboard and system case lights are on.

The Monitor

If the power supply checks out, the next thing to investigate is the monitor.

All modern monitors display a message or splash screen of some sort when switched on to indicate that they are functional. (Note that the monitor must be disconnected from the computer for this to work.)

Switch both monitor and computer off and then disconnect the cable from the video socket. If you're not sure which this is, simply follow the cable from the monitor to where it plugs in at the rear of the system case.

Switch the monitor back on (not the computer) and you should now see a message similar to the one below.

If you don't see a message and the monitor lights are off, then either the monitor itself is faulty or it's not getting any power. Check that there is power at the wall socket; check the power cord, the plug, the fuse and the connections. If these are all OK then the monitor must be faulty.

If you want to be absolutely sure before going out and buying a new monitor, the only conclusive test is to substitute it with one known to be good, or connect it to a different system.

Once you have eliminated the monitor, the next thing to check is the memory.

Memory

If your blank screen problem has appeared out of the blue and assuming the problem is memory related, the cause is almost certain to be faulty memory. If this is the case, you don't have many options.

The following are all you can do:

1) Check that the memory module is securely connected. Do this by opening the plastic retaining clips on either side of the memory socket to release the module. Pull it out and then reinsert it. The clips should close automatically

2) Remove the module as described above and install it into a different socket – memory sockets can become faulty

3) Replace the module

However, if the problem has come about as the result of a memory upgrade, you need to check several things. The first is that you have installed the memory in the correct slot, or slots. In most motherboards, when a single memory module is being used it must be installed in a particular slot, not just any one.

In the case of two or more modules installed in a dual- or triple-channel configuration, they may need to be installed in a certain order. Furthermore, many motherboards designed for this type of memory configuration will not work unless all the channels have a module installed in them, i.e. a triple-channel motherboard must have three modules.

Also, many of these motherboards provide two dual- or triple-channel circuits. The former will thus provide four memory slots – two for each circuit while the latter will provide six slots – three for each circuit. On these boards, the slots for each circuit will be a different color and if you are only going to use one of the circuits, the modules must be installed in the correct slots for that circuit.

Another problem that can be the result of a memory upgrade is buying modules that just don't work with the motherboard. Technically, they may be compatible but in practise the motherboard simply refuses to work with them, or vice versa. This issue can be avoided by making sure the memory you buy is recommended for use with the motherboard in your system.

Beware

Of all the parts in a PC that can be damaged by careless handling, memory modules are the most susceptible. You must ground yourself before handling these devices.

Hot tip

A classic symptom of incorrectly fitted memory modules is the PC continually starting and stopping within a second or two.

Hot tip

Information regarding which slots to use in the various types of memory configuration will be in the motherboard manual.

The Video System

With the power supply unit, monitor and memory eliminated, you are getting closer to finding the cause of your blank screen.

As we have seen in Chapter One, a PCs video is provided by either a dedicated video card or a video system integrated in the motherboard.

If you are using the former, the first thing to check is that it is securely connected to the motherboard. In the case of a PCI-Express video card, which requires a dedicated power supply from the PSU, make sure that this is present and correct. An operational video card cooling fan will confirm this.

Next check that the monitor is connected to the card. If your system has both integrated video and a video card, make sure the monitor is connected to the card and not the integrated video.

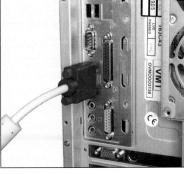

Video card   Integrated video

Hot tip

Note that when a video card is installed, it automatically disables integrated video. Therefore, if you are using an integrated video system to check the video card, you must first remove the video card from the system.

If you have both a video card and integrated video in your system, this provides a foolproof means of fault isolation. Remove the video card from the system and then connect the monitor to the integrated system. If you now have video, the issue lies with the video card.

If your computer doesn't have a video card then it is using an integrated system. In this situation, assuming all the other hardware devices check out, or a beep code indicates a video fault, you will need to either buy a new motherboard (as your video system is part and parcel of it), or buy a video card.

Motherboard and CPU

If your screen still remains stubbornly blank, the cause has to be a faulty motherboard or CPU. We'll start with the motherboard.

The first thing to check is that the connections for the system case's front panel on/off switch are OK – these are easily dislodged. You will find them in a small connection block at the bottom-right of the motherboard.

Assuming they are, the next thing to establish is whether the board is powered up. If any of the LEDs on the keyboard and front panel of the system case are lit, the board is receiving power. If not, remove the system case's side panel and check for any lit LEDs on the motherboard. If there aren't any, shut the PC down, ground yourself by touching the chassis briefly and then place a finger on the chipset's heatsink – this should be warm. If it isn't, the motherboard is not powered up.

Check that the board's power connector is pushed right in and, if it is, the problem will be that no power is coming from the power supply unit. While the PSU may give every appearance of being operational (warm to the touch, fan running), the internal circuit that provides the motherboard's power will be damaged. Replace the PSU.

If the board is receiving power, but the keyboard and system case LEDs are not lit, this is a sure sign that the board is faulty. However, if the board is powered up, and you can see that the above mentioned LEDs are working, this is an equally good sign that the motherboard is OK.

This leaves us with the CPU. Before you condemn it though, do check that the heatsink fan is operational. If it isn't, you've almost certainly found the cause of the problem as an overheating CPU will automatically shut down to prevent damage to itself. Remake the fan's power connection and if this doesn't do the trick, you will have to replace the fan.

If the fan is working, then the CPU is almost certainly faulty. The only way to establish this conclusively though, is to replace it.

However, as you have eliminated all other possible causes, you can be fairly sure that a new CPU will fix the problem.

Beep Codes

As we saw on page 24, beep codes are produced by a diagnostic utility built-in to the BIOS. Each of these codes are specific to a particular device and indicate that it has a problem. The table below shows the beep codes for AWARD and AMI BIOSs.

Hot tip

Because different BIOS manufacturers use different codes, you will first have to establish the manufacturer of the BIOS in your system – this information will be in the computer's manual.

Beeps	Fault
AWARD BIOS	
1 long, 2 short	Video system
Any other sequence	Memory
AMI BIOS	
1, 2 or 3	Memory
4, 6, 9, 10 or 11	Motherboard
5 or 7	CPU
8	Video system

Computer Boot Sequence

The following is a simplified version of a PC's boot sequence:

1) The computer is switched on
2) The motherboard powers up and initializes its components
3) The CPU starts running and initializes the BIOS
4) The BIOS checks the video system (after which the first boot screen appears)
5) The BIOS checks the memory (this check is visible on the first boot screen)
6) The BIOS checks the hard drive
7) The BIOS checks all other system hardware
8) The BIOS checks all the drives for the operating system
9) The operating system is loaded into the PC's memory
10) The operating system starts
11) The desktop appears on the screen

Hot tip

Knowing your PC's boot sequence is a very handy aid to hardware troubleshooting. If the PC's bootup stops at a particular stage, the hardware involved in the previous stages can be eliminated as a cause of the problem.

If any problems are encountered in steps 1 to 4, bootup stops with a blank screen. If bootup stops at the memory test (usually with an error message), the memory is faulty. If the BIOS can't find a hard drive, or can't find an operating system on it, bootup will stop with a "Disk Boot Failure" error message.

Bootup Doesn't Complete

Referring back to page 24, we saw that another type of boot problem is where the procedure starts but fails to finish. This is the more likely of the two scenarios, which is fortunate as it is also, usually, the less serious.

In this situation you will see text on the screen as the PC starts to boot. This indicates that the CPU, motherboard, video system and monitor are all functioning correctly.

The only two hardware devices that are likely to stop the boot procedure once started are the memory and the hard drive. Although very rare, other hardware such as USB flash drives, external hard drives and peripherals can cause this problem as well. For this reason, disconnect all these non-essential devices before going any further.

Operating system failure can also result in a failed boot – we look at this in Chapter Three.

Memory

This is simple to diagnose. Part of the BIOS's startup routine is the memory test or count. This establishes how much memory is installed in the computer. If bootup stops at this point, as shown below, the only possible cause is a faulty memory module. Troubleshoot as described on page 27.

Don't forget

Before troubleshooting hardware causes of a failed boot, remove all non-essential hardware from the system.

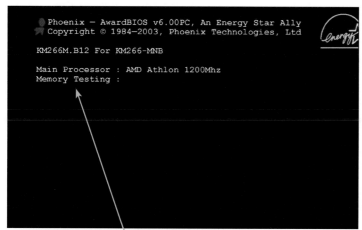

```
  Phoenix — AwardBIOS v6.00PC, An Energy Star Ally
  Copyright © 1984—2003, Phoenix Technologies, Ltd

  KM266M.B12 For KM266-MNB

  Main Processor : AMD Athlon 1200Mhz
  Memory Testing :
```

Bootup has stopped at the memory test

If the memory test is successful, the hard drive is the next thing to investigate.

...cont'd

Hard Drive

When you start the computer, on the first boot screen you should see the hard drive listed (the Samsung HD103SJ in the example below). If it is, this indicates that the BIOS has recognized the drive and configured it correctly.

If it isn't there, the BIOS isn't "seeing" it. Depending on the BIOS in your system, one of two things will happen:

1) Bootup will stop at this point

2) Bootup will continue and then stop with a "Disk Boot Failure" error message

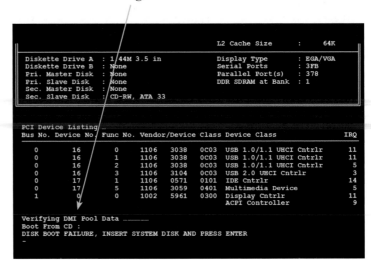

Either of these can be caused by four things:

1) The drive is not connected
2) The drive is not powered up
3) The system is configured to boot from a non-boot drive
4) The drive is faulty

The first thing to check is that the drive is connected to the motherboard. Remake the interface connections and check that they are correct.

Then check the drive is getting power from the power supply unit. The easiest way to do this is to connect a different power connector that you know is working; for example, the one powering the CD/DVD drive.

If both of the above check out, the system may be configured to boot from a non-boot drive. This is particularly likely if you have two or more hard drives in the system. Check this as follows:

Go into the BIOS (see top margin note), open the Advanced Features page, select "Hard Disk Boot Priority" and make sure the boot drive (the one Windows is installed on) is specified as the first drive.

Hot tip

To enter the BIOS program, boot the PC and on the first boot screen press the required key. This is usually the Delete key and will be specified at the bottom of the screen, and also in the motherboard manual.

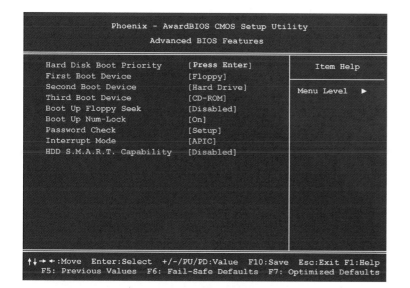

```
           Phoenix - AwardBIOS CMOS Setup Utility
                   Advanced BIOS Features

 Hard Disk Boot Priority     [Press Enter]        Item Help
 First Boot Device           [Floppy]
 Second Boot Device          [Hard Drive]       Menu Level   ►
 Third Boot Device           [CD-ROM]
 Boot Up Floppy Seek         [Disabled]
 Boot Up Num-Lock            [On]
 Password Check              [Setup]
 Interrupt Mode              [APIC]
 HDD S.M.A.R.T. Capability   [Disabled]




↑↓→←:Move  Enter:Select  +/-/PU/PD:Value  F10:Save  Esc:Exit F1:Help
   F5: Previous Values  F6: Fail-Safe Defaults  F7: Optimized Defaults
```

Don't forget

If you install two or more hard drives in your system, remember to check that the boot drive has priority in the BIOS. This is the drive in which the BIOS will expect to find the operating system.

If this checks out as well, your hard drive is faulty.

...cont'd

Another problem that can occur is the boot procedure stopping at the "Verifying DMI Pool Data" stage. DMI pool data is hardware related information that is passed from the BIOS to the operating system during bootup, and if the BIOS finds an error during the verification stage, the boot procedure may stop at this point.

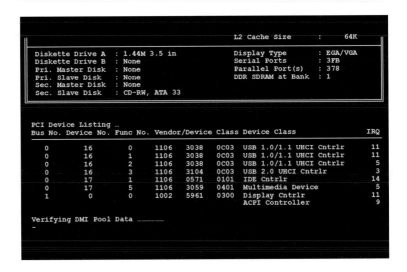

The usual cause is a connection problem but it can also be the result of a transient configuration issue that can be resolved by simply switching off and then back on again. This is the first thing to try. If the problem persists however, you almost certainly have a bad connection somewhere.

Operating System Failure

On page 31 we saw that operating system failure can also be the cause of the boot procedure stopping – this can happen when the operating system's startup files are corrupt and so prevent it being loaded into the memory. With Windows Vista and Windows 7 this is indicated by the following error message:

```
BOOTMGR is missing
Press Ctrl+Alt+Del to restart
_
```

Troubleshoot this issue as described on pages 36-41.

3 Windows

This chapter looks at issues that prevent Windows from starting. We also see how to restore an unrepairable Windows installation.

Windows won't Start

In Chapter Two we saw that one of the causes of PCs refusing to start is faulty hardware. In this chapter we look at another cause – a damaged Windows installation.

When this happens, the boot procedure will get to a certain point and then stop. You may get an error message or just a blank screen. No matter how many times you try, the result is the same.

The most common cause of this is exiting Windows incorrectly.

Instead of clicking Turn Off or Restart, you may have done one of the following:

- Pressed the PC's reset button

- Switched the computer off with the on/off button while Windows was running

- Crashed the computer

With any of these "exits" you run the risk of corrupting the operating system's startup files, or creating file system errors with the result that Windows may refuse to load on restart.

The first thing to check is the possibility of file system corruption and to do this you need to get back into Windows to run the disk checking utility Chkdsk.

The question is, how can you do it if you can't get into Windows in the first place?

Safe Mode

The answer is to start Windows in Safe Mode – see margin note. This is the Windows troubleshooting mode and is designed to get the system going if at all possible. To do it, reboot and keep tapping the F8 key until you see the Windows Advanced Options menu. Using the arrow keys, scroll to Safe Mode and press Enter.

```
Windows Advanced Options Menu
Please select An Option

Safe Mode
Safe Mode With Networking
Safe Mode With Command Prompt

Enable Boot Logging
Enable VGA Mode
Last Known Good Configuration (Yout Most Recent Settings That Worked)
Directory Services Restore Mode (Windows Domain Controllers Only)

Start Windows Normally
Reboot
Return To OS Choices Menu

Use the up and down arrow keys to move the highlight to your choice
```

Hot tip

Safe Mode works by bypassing the normal Windows configuration, and instead loading a minimum set of basic drivers. This eliminates a number of issues that might prevent the operating system from starting and will usually get you back into Windows from where you can find and fix the problem.

Windows should now start. It will take longer than normal so give it time. You will also find that while in Safe Mode, it will run a lot slower and many of its functions will be disabled.

When Windows is running in Safe Mode, go to My Computer and right-click the hard drive icon. Click Properties and then open the Tools tab. Under Error-checking, click the Check Now... button. In the dialog box that opens, click Start. You will now get a message saying that the disk cannot be checked while it is in use. Click "Schedule disk check" and then click OK.

Restart the PC, and just before the point when Windows usually loads, Chkdsk will start. The utility will scan your hard drive for file system errors and if it finds any, it will repair them. The PC will then reboot automatically.

```
Checking file system on C:
The type of the file system is NTFS.

A disk check has been scheduled.
windows will now check the disk.

CHKDSK is verifying files (stage 1 of 3)...
```

If Windows now starts, congratulations – you've resolved the problem.

System Restore

If Chkdsk doesn't do the trick then you have a more serious problem, which may require a reinstallation of Windows. However, before going to these lengths, a Windows utility known as System Restore may provide the answer.

This utility automatically takes snapshots, known as "restore points", of the system when major changes are made to it. These restore points can subsequently be used to restore the system to the state it was in when the restore point was made.

Note that these restore points are not mirror images of the system but rather a backup of certain Windows system files, programs, registry settings and executable files.

Use it to restore your system as described below:

1. Reboot the PC into Safe Mode

2. When Windows is running, go to Start, All Programs, Accessories, System Tools, System Restore

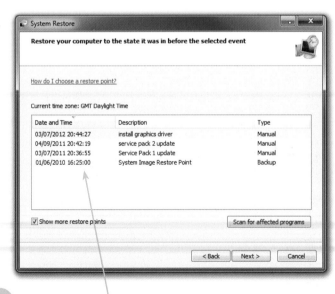

3. Choose a restore point made on a day when the PC was known to be working

The PC will now be restored to the state it was in when the restore point was made.

Windows Startup Repair

If System Restore doesn't resolve the issue then you have a badly damaged Windows installation. Also, if you have attempted the Chkdsk procedure described on page 37 but were unable to get the PC running in Safe Mode, or to access System Restore as described on page 38, again the cause will be damage to Windows.

While having to do a reinstallation of Windows is becoming increasingly likely, you have three more options before this will be necessary.

The first involves a Windows utility called Startup Repair, which replaces the files used to start Windows with good copies. Because the utility and the good startup files are on the installation disk, you have to set the PC to boot from said disk to be able to access them. This is done in the BIOS as described below:

1 Reboot and go into the BIOS setup program (see top margin note). Use the arrow keys to select Advanced BIOS Features and then scroll down to First Boot Device

```
                Phoenix - AwardBIOS CMOS Setup Utility
                        Advanced BIOS Features

   Virus Warning                [Disabled]          Item Help
   CPU Internal Cache           [Enabled]
   External Cache               [Enabled]
   CPU L2 Cache ECC Checking     [Enabled]          Menu Level
   Quick Power On Self Test      [Enabled]
   First Boot Device            [CDROM]             Select Your
   Second Boot Device           [HDD-0]             Boot Device
   Third Boot Device            [Floppy]            Priority
   Boot Other Device            [Enabled]
   Swap Floppy Drive            [Disabled]
   Boot Up Floppy Seek          [Enabled]
   Boot Up NumLock Status       [On]
   Gate A20 Option              [Fast]
   Typematic Rate Setting       [Disabled]
 x Typematic Rate (Chars/Sec)    6
 x Typematic Delay (Msec)        250
   Security Option              [Setup]
   OS Select For DRAM > 64MB    [Non-OS2]
   HDD S.M.A.R.T. Capability    [Enabled]

   Enter:Select  +/-/PU/PD:Value  F10:Save ESC:Exit   F1:General Help
   F5  Previous Values   F6: Fail-Safe Defaults  F7: Optimized Defaults
```

2 Using the Page Up/Page Down keys, select CDROM. Save your changes (see margin note) and exit the BIOS

Hot tip

To enter the BIOS, boot the PC and on the first boot screen press the required key. This is usually the Delete key and will be specified at the bottom of the screen, and also in the motherboard manual.

Don't forget

When making a change in the BIOS you must save it before exiting the program, otherwise the setting will revert to the original. The option to do this is on the main BIOS page.

...cont'd

3 Now place the Windows installation disk in the CD/ DVD drive and boot the computer. After a few moments you will see a message saying "Press any key to boot from CD..." Do so and when the files have loaded, you will see the Windows installation screen – click Next

4 In the screen that opens, click "Repair my computer" and in the screen after that, click Next. Now you will see the System Recovery Options screen as shown below

Hot tip

If your Windows installation is severely damaged it is possible that you won't see the System Recovery Options screen as shown right. Instead, you will get an error message that says no operating system has been found. In this situation, you will have to reinstall Windows as described on pages 68-70.

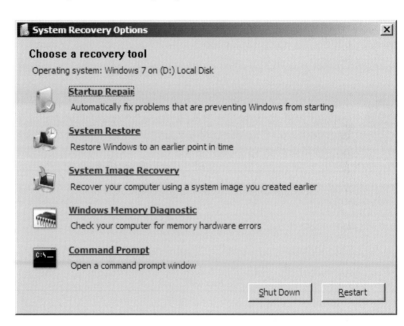

5 Select Startup Repair and click Next

Note that Startup Repair can only repair files needed to start Windows – it does nothing else.

If repairs aren't successful, you'll see a summary of the problem and links to contact information for support.

This utility can take a long time to run and doesn't provide a progress bar so you are never quite sure that it is actually doing anything. However, if the issue preventing Windows from starting is corrupted startup files, it will fix them – just be patient.

System File Checker

The next option is to try and repair any other Windows files that may be damaged or missing. This involves running a little known Windows utility known as the System File Checker.

It works by comparing every Windows file in the installation against the files held on the installation disk. If it finds any that are missing, or different (corrupted), it automatically replaces them from the disk. Proceed as follows:

1 Go to the System Recovery Options menu as described on page 40

2 Click Command Prompt to open the dialog box shown below

The System File Checker is primarily intended as a means of repairing the "every day" type of problems that can crop up in Windows.

Hot tip

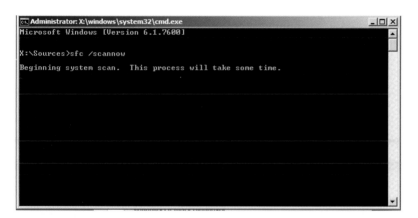

```
Administrator: X:\windows\system32\cmd.exe

Microsoft Windows [Version 6.1.7600]

X:\Sources>sfc /scannow

Beginning system scan.  This process will take some time.
```

3 Type sfc /scannow and then press Enter

The utility will now run. When it is finished, reboot the PC to see if the problem has been resolved.

Note that even if the System File Checker does find and repair any damaged files, it doesn't necessarily mean that Windows will now start. If the installation is seriously damaged, or the problem is a configuration issue, it probably won't. However, it is worth a try.

Restore Windows

Your final option is to restore a working copy of Windows from a previously made image backup. This will have been saved by Windows on a separate backup medium, e.g. a second hard drive when the image was created.

Assuming you have made an image, proceed as follows:

1. Access the System Recovery Options menu as described on page 40

2. Select System Image Recovery and click Next. The utility will now search your hard drives for Windows image files. If it finds one, it will select this automatically but if it finds two or more, it will select the most recent one

Beware

Any changes made to the PC's settings, and data created after the image was made, will be lost when the system is restored.

42

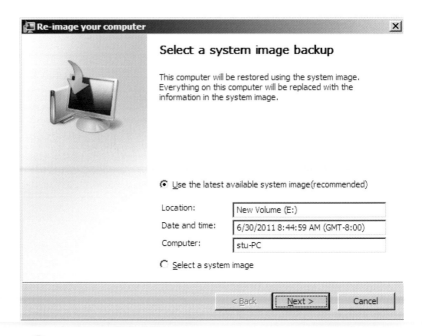

3. If you have more than one image file, you can also select it manually by checking "Select a system image". Then click Next

4 At the additional restore options screen, click Next

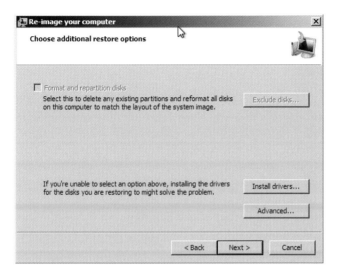

5 At the confirmation screen, click Finish

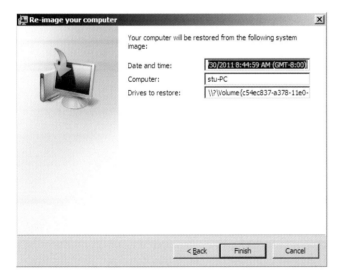

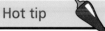

Hot tip

Creating an image of your system, and restoring it, only takes a few minutes. Creating a new image periodically will give you the security of knowing that what ever software related disaster may occur, a quick and easy way of resolving it is always at hand.

You will now see a message warning that all data on the drive will be deleted. Ignore this by clicking Next and the procedure will begin. First the drive will be reformatted, which destroys all the data on it and then the Windows installation will be recreated from the image file.

Windows is Unrepairable

If the procedures described haven't got Windows going then you have come to the end of the line – your Windows installation is unrepairable. The only course of action now is to install a new one.

However, you will almost certainly have data on your damaged installation that you don't want to lose. If you have it all backed up – fine, but what if you haven't? How can you get at your data to save it if you can't get into Windows in the first place?

The good news is that you don't have to. We explain how to install Windows 7 on pages 68-70 so we won't repeat it here, but what you have to do is simply go through the installation procedure as though you were starting from scratch, i.e installing a new copy of Windows on a new hard drive.

What will happen is that at the beginning of the installation routine, Windows will see that an existing installation exists (the damaged one) and show you the following message:

Hot tip

Another way of getting at and backing up your data is to use the Command Prompt option in the System Recovery Options menu, as shown on page 41. This is a powerful tool that enables the user to do many things including backing up either the entire system, or selected files and folders. However, using it is far from easy and beyond the remit of this book to explain.

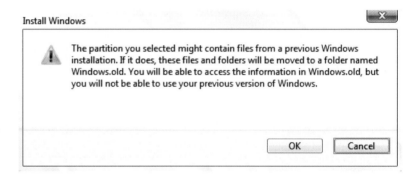

This tells you that the data from the existing installation will be moved to a folder named Windows.old. Just click OK and let the new installation complete.

When it has, go to your hard drive (Windows (C:) in My Computer and open it. You will now see the Windows.old folder, which contains all the data from the damaged installation.

Browse through it and copy all the data you want to keep to a new location. When you have finished, simply delete the Windows.old folder.

4 Performance

A computer that takes ages to do anything is a serious pain in the neck. In this chapter, we look at issues that can cause a PC to under-perform. For example, how to check that your hardware is up-to-scratch. We also show you some tips that will boost your PC's performance.

Why is My PC Slow?

Inadequate Hardware

There are many things that can cause a PC to run slower than normal and, as many users have discovered, one of the most common is upgrading the operating system. This is because modern operating systems are very resource intensive and so require powerful hardware.

Of these, the ones that have the most impact on performance are the Central Processing Unit (CPU) and the memory (RAM). If you are running Windows 7 or Windows Vista, the video system is also important.

So how do you know if your hardware is adequate? We'll take a look at the requirements for Windows 7 as this is the latest operating system, and also the most demanding of all in terms of hardware requirements.

The minimum required to run Windows 7 is a CPU rated at a speed of 1 GHz, 1 GB of memory, and a DirectX 9 capable video system. However, while it may run, it won't do so particularly well.

To get good performance from this operating system, you will need a CPU of at least 2.0 GHz, 2 GB of memory, and a video system that has a minimum of 128 MB integral memory and that is capable of supporting DirectX 9.

Details of your CPU, the memory and video system can be obtained from the System Information utility. Click Start, All Programs, Accessories, System Tools, System Information.

Hot tip

Older PCs that use an integrated video system, or a low-end video card, may be restricted to the Basic interface when upgrading to Windows Vista or Windows 7. Owners of these PCs who wish to run the Aero interface may need to upgrade their video systems.

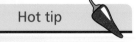

Hot tip

The System Information utility tells you a lot of other things about your system as well.

On the system summary page, look down the Item column.

Next to Processor and Total Physical Memory are details of the CPU and memory respectively.

Next, click the Components category on the left and then click Display. In the Item column, next to Adaptor RAM are details of the video system's integral memory capacity.

To find out the version of DirectX installed on your PC, type Dxdiag.exe in the Start Menu search box. Then press Enter to open the DirectX utility.

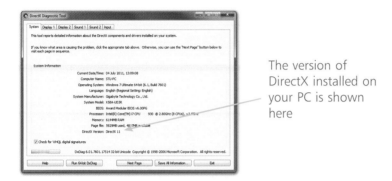

The version of DirectX installed on your PC is shown here

Windows 7 users also have a simpler way of evaluating their system's hardware. Go to Start, Control Panel and click Performance Information and Tools.

Hot tip

For general PC use (word processing, Internet, etc), a subscore of two is adequate. For graphic-intensive applications, such as PC games and video editing, a rating of three to four will be required. If the rating of any part is less than two, you should upgrade it with a more capable model.

This utility shows the major parts in your PC together with a performance rating (under the Subscore column) – see margin note.

...cont'd

Fragmented Hard Drive

Fragmentation is a term used to describe the way that files saved to a hard drive have their data split up on different parts of the drive's disk, or disks, instead of being stored contiguously. When a fragmented file is accessed the drive's read/write heads have to hunt about to locate all the different parts of it before they can be reassembled in the original form. The result is that the file will take much longer to open than it should do, and the system will consequently be sluggish.

To address this issue, Windows provides a tool called Disk Defragmenter. This application "undoes" the fragmentation by rearranging the data on the disk so that each file is stored as a complete unit.

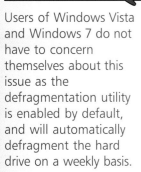
1   Go to Start, All Programs, Accessories, System Tools

2   Select the hard drive and click Defragment disk

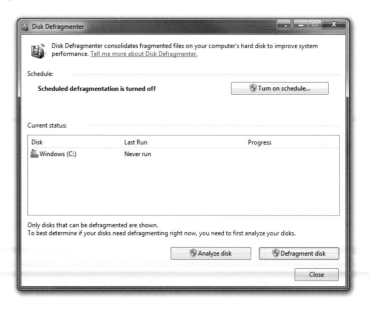

With a well used PC, it is good practice to defragment your hard drive about once a month. Otherwise every 3 or 4 months will be quite adequate.

It is important that you do this, as a severely fragmented drive will affect the performance of a PC drastically.

Program Overload

The next thing to look at is the number of programs you have on your PC. The more there are, the slower it is going to be, even if they are not being used. If this puzzles you, be aware that many applications (or parts of them) run unseen in the background even if they appear to be closed.

A typical example is CD/DVD authoring programs: these usually install a virtual CD driver that runs even when the program is closed. Many other programs do the same sort of thing.

So the more software you install, inevitably the more of these background applications there will be. Not only do they slow system performance, they also affect shutdown and startup speeds.

The solution is to go through your hard drive and uninstall all programs that you don't need – if you're like most people, there will probably be dozens of them. Do this as described below:

1 Click Start, Control Panel, Programs and Features

2 Here you will see a list of all the programs that have been installed on the computer

Go through the list and uninstall all the ones you can live without. The more you can get rid of, the better the overall performance of your PC will be.

Hot tip

Keep an eye on how much of your hard drive's space has been used. When it approaches 70%, its performance and thus the PC's, will start to decrease.

...cont'd

Corrupted File System

Over time, especially if the PC is well used, file system and data faults can build up on the hard drive. Not only can these have an adverse effect on the PC's performance, they can also be the cause of general system instability, and thus potential loss of data.

To correct these types of fault, Windows provides a disk checking utility called Chkdsk. Check your system with it as follows:

1 Open My Computer and right-click the hard drive. Click Properties and then the Tools tab

Hot tip

Make a point of running Chkdsk on a regular basis. In particular, be sure to run it after every incorrect shutdown or system crash. These actions are likely to introduce file system errors to the hard drive. If you don't do this, one of these days your system will simply refuse to start.

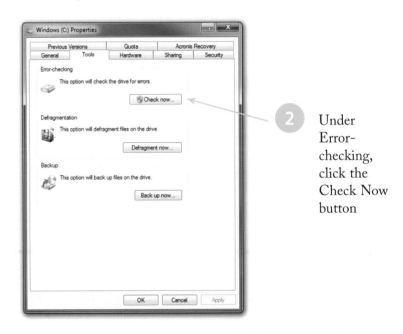

2 Under Error-checking, click the Check Now button

3 Check "Automatically fix file system errors". Then click Start

Note that running Chkdsk on the drive on which Windows is installed will require a system reboot. With all other drives, the procedure is done while Windows is running.

Registry Errors

The registry is a central database that holds all the important Windows settings regarding software, hardware, and system configuration. It also provides a common location where all applications can save their launching parameters and data.

Over time, as the user installs and deletes programs, creates shortcuts and changes system settings, etc, obsolete and invalid information builds up in the registry. While this does not have a major impact on a PC's performance, it can be the cause of system and program errors that can lead to instability issues.

The solution is to scan the registry periodically with a suitable application that will locate all the invalid entries and delete them.

While Windows Registry Editor is adequate for editing purposes, it does not provide a cleaning option. However, there are many of these applications available for download from the Internet. One that we recommend is CCleaner (shown below). This is a free program and, as with others of its type, provides various options such as full or selective scans, backups, the creation of System Restore points, etc.

Running a registry cleaner once every month or so will help to keep your system stable, and thus more reliable.

51

Beware

Changes to the registry can be dangerous. So use the registry cleaner's backup option to create a backup first. If you have any problems as a result of the changes, you will be able to undo them by restoring the original settings.

Hot tip

We recommend you clean the registry about once a month. However, if you frequently install and uninstall software, change system settings, etc, it will be worth doing it more often.

Performance Tips

Add More Memory

Without any doubt, the quickest and most effective method of improving the overall performance of a computer is to simply increase the amount of memory it has.

So how do you go about doing this? It is in fact, a very simple procedure that takes no more than a few minutes but does require the system case to be opened. Once this has been done, you will see a large circuit board facing you at the right-hand side of the case. This is the motherboard and at the top-right, you will see the memory sockets containing the memory modules as shown below:

Hot tip

To find out how much memory your PC has, right-click the My Computer icon on the Start menu and then click Properties. Memory capacity will be detailed in the System section.

Don't forget

You cannot install just any memory - it has to be compatible. Consult your PC's manual to see which type you need.

Open the retaining clips and insert the new module by pressing down on the top edge until the retaining clips close automatically

Hot tip

Memory modules must be handled very carefully. Before touching one, ground yourself by touching the case chassis. If you don't, the electrostatic electricity in your body could well damage it.

If one or more of the sockets are empty all you have to do is fit extra modules to complement the existing ones. If the sockets are all in use, you will have to remove some, or all, of the modules and replace them with modules of a larger capacity.

Before you go and buy more memory for your system, make sure it is the right type. If your PC is no more than five years or so old, it will almost certainly be using DDR2 memory, but do check. Consult the PC's manual to see exactly what type is required.

ReadyBoost

Mechanical hard drives read small data files much faster that they do large ones. Flash memory as used in USB flash drives, on the other hand, is much faster than a hard drive at reading small files but slower at reading large files.

A Windows 7 feature known as ReadyBoost makes use of this flash memory characteristic. When it is enabled on a USB flash drive, ReadyBoost uses the drive as a memory cache for the reading of small files. However, when a large file is being read, in which case the flash drive will be slower than the hard drive, ReadyBoost is turned off and the file is read from the hard drive.

This feature can improve the performance of a PC considerably. To use it, connect a USB flash drive to your system and the ReadyBoost option will appear as shown below:

Beware

ReadyBoost will not work with a flash drive unless it is capable of reading data at 2.5 MBps and writing it at 1.75 MBps. So when buying a flash drive for this purpose, check its specifications.

53

1 Click "Speed up my system"

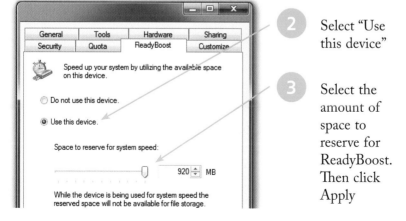

2 Select "Use this device"

3 Select the amount of space to reserve for ReadyBoost. Then click Apply

Hot tip

The minimum amount of flash memory you can use with ReadyBoost is 256 MB and the maximum amount is 4 GB. With Windows Vista ReadyBoost can only be used on one USB drive, whereas with Windows 7, up to 8 drives can be used.

Note that a ReadyBoost enabled flash drive does not increase the amount of memory in the PC – it increases the speed at which data is accessed.

Reduce the Visual Effects

Windows comes with a number of visual effects, e.g. fading or sliding menus, drop shadows, pointer shadows, etc. These are all designed to improve the look and feel of the Windows interface. However, they add nothing to its functionality. In fact they can, and do, have a negative impact on the system. Remember: each of these effects consumes system resources.

Users interested in, or needing, performance rather than appearance will benefit from disabling some, or even all, of these essentially unnecessary graphic enhancements. Do it as follows:

Click Start, Control Panel, System, Advanced system settings. Then click the Settings button under Performance.

On the Visual Effects tab you will see a list of all Windows visual effects, plus several user options. By default, Windows chooses the first option and invariably enables the majority, if not all, of the effects.

To disable an effect just uncheck its box. The question is, though, which ones do you disable?

The effects that have the greatest impact on performance are:

- Show shadows under menus

- Use a background image for each folder type

- Use visual styles on windows and buttons

- Use drop shadows for icon labels on the Desktop

- Show thumbnails instead of icons

For maximum performance gain, disable all the effects. Otherwise, disable just the ones in the list above.

Beware

Disabling all of the effects will have a significant impact on the appearance of Windows.

The PC is Slow to Start

This is a common problem that is often caused by simply having too much software installed on the PC – see page 49. Another cause is having a number of programs that automatically start with Windows so that they are open and ready to use when, or shortly after, the Desktop appears.

These programs are located in the Startup folder: they can be placed here by the user if he or she wants them to open with Windows. Also, some programs will automatically place a link here when they are installed.

As each of these programs must be loaded before Windows is ready for use, the more there are in the Startup folder, the longer startup will take. Check it out as follows:

see page 49

1 Click Start, All Programs, Startup

2 In the Startup folder, you'll see a list of applications that start with Windows. Remove any that you don't need by right-clicking and then clicking Delete

Beware

The more programs you have in your Startup folder, the longer the PC will take to start.

Hot tip

Another way of finding out which programs are in the Startup folder is via the System Information utility. This is accessible from Start, All Programs, Accessories, System Tools.

However, clearing out the Startup folder is only half the battle. You now have to find and get rid of the startup programs that run unseen in the background, and thus aren't so obvious.

1 Type msconfig in the Start menu's search box and press Enter. This opens the System Configuration utility. Click the Startup tab

56

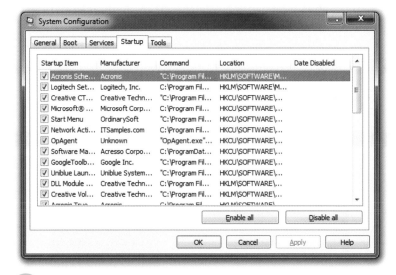

2 Here you will see a list of more programs that start with Windows

To disable a program, simply uncheck it. You can, in fact, quite safely disable all of them by clicking the Disable All button – none of them plays any critical role (if they did, there wouldn't be a Disable All button).

However, we would suggest that you refrain from disabling your antivirus program, which will be listed here (assuming you have one). This application plays an essential role in keeping your system free of viruses.

The PC is Slow to Shutdown

When the shutdown button is pressed, Windows attempts to close all running applications and services before initiating the shutdown. If an application refuses to close, or takes its time to do so, Windows will wait a specified period before forcibly terminating it.

The first thing you can try is to reduce the time Windows waits.

1 Click Start and in the search box type: regedit and then press Enter. This will open the registry editor

2 Expand the hierarchical tree at the left and browse to HKEY_LOCAL_MACHINE\System\ CurrentControlSet\Control. Click the Control folder and on the right of the dialog box you'll see an entry called WaitToKillServiceTimeout

3 Right-click on WaitToKillServiceTimeout and then click Modify. In the Edit String dialog box, lower the default setting of 12000 to 2000

Reboot the PC and from now on Windows will wait for 2 seconds before closing applications instead of the 12 seconds it was previously.

Windows also provides a utility known as the Event Log that monitors various processes, which includes the shutdown procedure. Any issues that interfere with a smooth shutdown are logged.

Access the Event Log as follows:

1 Go to Start, Control Panel, Performance Information and Tools

2 On the left-hand side, click Advanced Tools and then click "View performance details in Event log"

At the top of the window in the middle, there will be various warning and error alerts. Under Task Category on the right, you'll see that they relate mainly to boot and shutdown issues.

Click any entries regarding shutdown problems and below, in the main part of the window, you'll see details of the problem. In the example above, the author's email program, Outlook, has caused a delay in the shutdown process.

The Event log can also be used to find problems that slow down the PC's bootup procedure.

5 Installation

Here, we look at problems typically encountered when installing software and hardware devices. We also see how to install Windows.

A Program won't Install

Installing a program is usually very simple – insert the installation disk in the CD/DVD drive and an installation screen will appear, as shown in the example below.

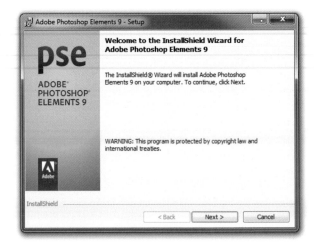

60

However, for a number of reasons this may not always happen. With no installation screen, how do you install the program? The solution is as follows:

1 Go to Start, My Computer

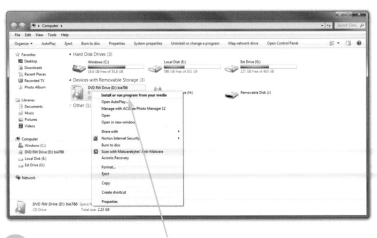

2 Right-click the CD/DVD drive and click "Install or run program..."

A Program won't Run

When you install programs on your PC, you may come across one or two that refuse to run: this will be because they were designed for an earlier version of Windows.

The solution is the Windows Program Compatibility Assistant. You can use this in two ways:

The first, and easiest, method is to right-click the program's setup file and click Properties at the bottom of the right-click menu.

Then open the Compatibility tab. Check the "Run this program in compatibility mode for:" checkbox.

From the drop-down list, select an earlier Windows version, or one you know the program is compatible with, and then click Apply and OK.

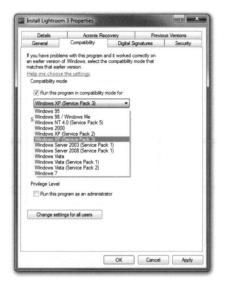

Hot tip

Once a program has been successfully set up, it will automatically use the compatibility settings every time it is run.

61

Then try running the program again; this time it should work.

The second way is to right-click the program's setup file as above but this time, click "Troubleshoot compatibility" as shown left.

Then simply follow the prompts. Windows will apply compatibility settings it thinks will work and then attempt to run the program. If it does, close it and select "Yes, set this program to always use these compatibility settings".

Click Next, and you're done.

However, while the Windows Compatibility Assistant will get most programs running, it isn't guaranteed to work with all. In this situation there is another option – a virtual PC.

This requires a program that creates a virtual PC environment on a physical (host) PC. Once created, any operating system can be installed on the virtual PC. So if you're running Windows 7 and have a program that only worked on Windows 98, for example, you can install a copy of Windows 98 on the virtual PC and then install the program on that. Essentially, it's a PC within a PC.

If the program that won't run requires Windows XP, you can download a virtual copy of this from www.microsoft.com/windows/virtual-pc/download.aspx. The download also includes a copy of Microsoft's Windows Virtual PC program. Run the XP Mode setup file and a virtual PC will be created on your computer with Windows XP as the operating system. Then install the program that is incompatible with the host operating system.

Hot tip

A virtual PC can also be used to run hardware. For example, you may have an old scanner that only works with Windows XP because the manufacturer hasn't updated the scanner's driver so that it is compatible with later versions of Windows.

62

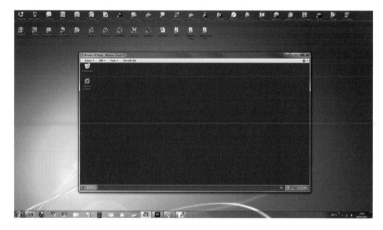

A virtual Windows XP installation running on a Windows 7 PC

If you wish to run a virtual operating system other than XP on Microsoft's Windows Virtual PC, you will have to download the standalone version.

There are many other virtual PC programs as well. One we recommend is VirtualBox. This is a free application, which you can get at www.oracle.com/technetwork/server-storage/virtualbox/downloads/index.html. Any operating system can be installed on this program.

A Program won't Uninstall

This is a common problem, and is usually caused by uninstalling the program in question incorrectly. This mistake is often made in one of two ways:

- Right-clicking the program in the All Programs menu and clicking Delete

- Right-clicking the program in the Program Files folder and clicking Delete

With the former, all you are doing is deleting a shortcut that leads to the program's location in the Program Files folder.

With the latter, while you will delete the program's files, you will not delete any configuration changes the program has made to the system's settings. As a result, it is not completely uninstalled and thus may still be having an effect on the system.

The correct way to uninstall a program is as follows:

1 Go to Start, Control Panel

2 Click Programs and Features

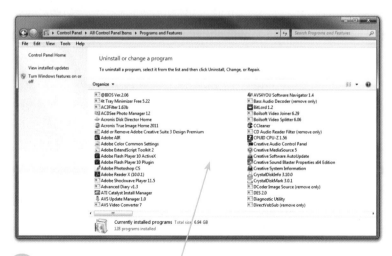

3 Select the program from the list, right-click it and click Uninstall

Hot tip

If you have already deleted a program's files from the Program Files folder, you may be unable to delete it correctly as described here. In this case, you will have to reinstall the program and then uninstall it in the correct manner.

A Device Won't Install

You've installed a new hardware device on your system but it doesn't work. There are two likely causes:

Missing Device Driver

You have not installed the device's driver. This will be on the installation disk provided with the device. Place this in the CD/DVD drive and, when the installation screen appears, click the Install button.

The driver tells Windows that its associated device is there and what it needs in the way of system resources. In most cases you will then have to reboot the PC to complete the installation.

When you are back in Windows, the device should then be operational. However, some devices – printers, scanners, and cable modems being typical examples – often require the driver to be installed *before* the device is connected to the PC.

If you've done the opposite, disconnect the device from the PC, uninstall the driver and then do it the correct way.

Bad or Incorrect Connections

Having made sure that the device has been installed correctly, if it still doesn't work then you have a connection issue.

If it's a peripheral device, such as a scanner or a printer, it will almost certainly be using a USB connection. Check that the connection is good and then try connecting the device to a different USB socket (it's not unheard-of for a socket to be faulty).

If it is connected via a USB hub, bypass the hub by connecting the device directly to a USB port on the PC. If it now works the hub is either faulty or is itself connected to a bad USB port.

In the case of an expansion card, such as a sound or video card, check that the card is pushed home in its socket. If the card also has a cable connection to the system, as video cards have (to the monitor), check that this is connected correctly.

With regard to video cards, models that use the PCI-Express interface require a separate power supply from the power supply unit. This will be in the form of a 4- or 6-pin connector. Make sure you have connected this.

Another common mistake made with both video and sound cards is to connect the monitor (in the case of video cards) and the speakers (in the case of sound cards) to the video or sound system provided by the motherboard.

Don't forget

If your system has both integrated video and a video card, check that you have connected the monitor to the correct system.

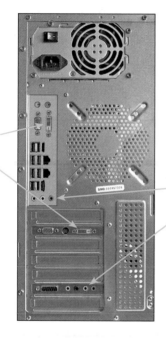

The monitor should be connected not to the integrated video system but to the video card

The speakers should be connected not to the integrated sound system but to the sound card

Getting the speaker connections wrong is also easily done. They must be connected as shown below:

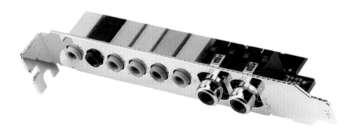

A two-speaker system connects to the green socket. With a multiple-speaker system, the green socket is used for the front speakers, the black socket for the rear speakers, and the orange sockets for the center and side speakers

Hot tip

Most sound cards provide color-coded input and output jacks for easy identification.

Green – line out
Orange – line out
Black – line out
Blue – line in
Pink – microphone

A New Hard Drive isn't Recognized

You've installed a new hard drive but your system isn't "seeing" it, i.e. it isn't listed in My Computer. The first thing to check is that it has been recognized by the BIOS. Do this by rebooting the PC and on the first boot screen, your drive should be listed.

If it isn't, it has a connection or power issue. Check the drive is powered up and make sure the interface connection is good. If the problem persists, it will be because the drive hasn't been partitioned and formatted.

These two procedures vary according to which version of Windows you are using and also on whether the drive is to be used purely for extra storage or is going to be the main system drive, i.e. where Windows is installed.

Assuming the drive is to be used for extra storage, proceed as follows:

1 Go to Start, Control Panel, Administrative Tools

2 Click Computer Management and then on the left-hand side, click Disk Management

3 After a few moments, the following window will appear

4 This shows all the drives in the system and your new drive (Disk 0 in the screenshot above) will be listed here

---

Don't forget

When you install a new hard drive, it must be partitioned and formatted before it can be used.

Hot tip

Drives can be split into a number of partitions, each of which appear to the operating system as a separate hard drive. Alternatively, one partition equal to the entire capacity of the drive can be created (this is the usual setup).

5 Right-click the drive and click New Simple Volume (volume is Microsoft parlance for a partition). Windows New Simple Volume Wizard will open. Click Next

6 Click Next in the two dialog boxes that follow

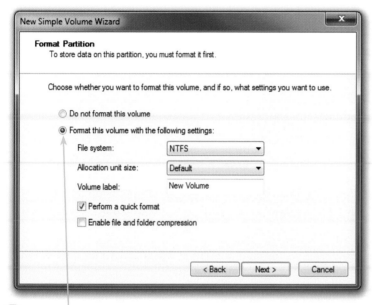

Hot tip

Partitioning is the process of defining specific areas of the hard disk for the operating system to use. Formatting prepares a disk to receive data by organizing it into logical units called blocks, sectors and tracks. These enable the drive's read/write heads to accurately position and locate data.

7 Select "Format this volume..." and click Next. Windows will now partition and format the drive. When the procedure is complete, the drive will be available for use

If you now go to My Computer, you will see the drive listed there. If the above procedure is not done the drive won't be recognized by the system and will not show in My Computer.

If the drive is to be used as the boot drive, i.e. the drive Windows is installed on, the partitioning and formatting procedures cannot be done from Windows. In this case, you have to use the partitioning/formatting tools on the Windows installation disk.

This is part and parcel of the Windows installation procedure, as described on page 68-70.

Installing Windows

In Chapter Three, we looked at various methods of repairing a damaged Windows installation. If none of them has worked for you, the only option left is to do a new installation as described below:

1 Set the system to boot from the CD/DVD drive as explained on page 39

2 Place the Windows installation disk in the drive and boot the PC

3 When you see a message saying "press any key to boot from CD...", do so

Windows will now load its installation files from the disk. You will then see the following screen:

4 Select the required language, and time and currency format, and then click Next. In the next dialog box, click the "Install Now" button.

5 OK the licence agreement

6 For the type of installation, select the Custom (advanced) option

7 In the "Where do you want to install Windows?" screen, you'll see your unformatted and unpartitioned hard drive. Click Drive options (advanced) – see bottom margin note

...cont'd

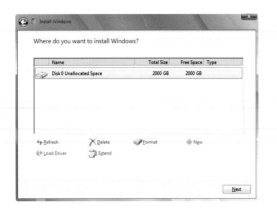

8 Click New

Hot tip

At step 9, Windows automatically creates a partition equal to the total capacity of the drive. However, you have the option of creating two or more partitions by entering a lower number in the "Size" box and then clicking New. The maximum size of a second partition will be the difference between the size of the first partition and the total capacity of the drive, and so on.

9 Click Apply to create a single partition equal to the size of the drive

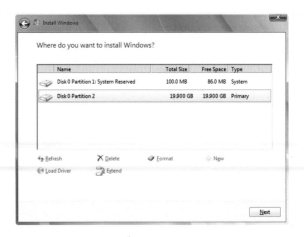

Click Next, and the Windows installation procedure will begin. It should take between 10 and 30 minutes to complete depending on the speed of your PC.

6 Video and Sound

Sound and video problems are very common. Video issues range from no video at all to unintelligible displays, while sound faults are usually a result of incorrect connections. This chapter shows how to resolve these issues.

No Display

If your monitor is blank from the point of switching the PC on, i.e. you don't even get a boot screen, you have a hardware issue – troubleshoot as described in Chapter Two.

If the PC boots but the screen goes blank at the point where Windows begins to load, the problem is software related.

Video Driver

The most likely suspect is a corrupt or misconfigured video card driver so check this out first. Reboot the PC into Safe Mode as described on page 37 – this should get you back into Windows.

Then go to Start, Control Panel, Device Manager.

Hot tip

If your PC is using an integrated video system, the video driver will be on the disk supplied with the motherboard. If you have a separate video card, the driver will be on the disk supplied with the card.

Expand the Display adaptors category and you should see your video card listed as shown above. If so, right-click it and then click Uninstall. Then simply reinstall the video driver from the installation disk.

If the card isn't listed, again, reinstall the driver. Another option that essentially does the same thing is to use the System Restore utility to "roll" the system back to a working configuration.

Hardware Conflicts

If the problem persists, then you almost certainly have a hardware conflict. Note that this is not a hardware fault but rather a software issue in that the driver (which is software) for a different hardware device is probably interfering with the video card and preventing it from working.

For example, you may have a TV tuner card in the PC and the system is trying to run the video card from the tuner's driver. This is a tricky situation to be in as there is no way of knowing which device is causing the problem. Therefore the only thing you can do is to disconnect every non-essential hardware device from the system, e.g. printer, scanner, all expansion cards (except the video card), USB devices, DVD drives and external hard drives. The PC should be in a "bare bones" condition when you've finished.

Then you need to boot into Safe Mode, go to the Device Manager and uninstall the drivers (as shown on the previous page) for all the devices you have disconnected from the PC.

When you've done all this, start the PC up and see what happens. If the problem has been resolved, which it almost certainly will have been, all you have to do is reinstall your hardware one by one, rebooting each time until the problem returns. If it does, you'll know which device is the culprit. You may, however, find that the acts of remaking the physical connections and installing new copies of all the devices drivers have resolved the issue.

In the extremely unlikely event that you are still staring unhappily at a blank screen though, you have a faulty power supply unit – this is the only thing that's left. While it may be running, it will be damaged internally and, as a result, its current output will be below the level needed by the power-hungry devices in the PC; namely, the CPU and video card. Replace it.

Power Management

Now lets look at another scenario that can also be the cause of a blank monitor. Most users will be familiar with a Windows feature known as the Advanced Configuration and Power Interface (ACPI). This is a power saving feature that places the PC in standby mode (in which the monitor is blanked) after a given period of inactivity with the purpose of saving power. While intended primarily for use with laptops where battery conservation is an important issue, it is also enabled by default on most desktop PCs.

To "wake" the PC up all you have to do is click the mouse or press a key. This is fine when it works. But when the PC doesn't respond to any amount of mouse clicking or key bashing, again, you are in a tricky situation.

73

Hot tip

Should it prove necessary to replace the power supply unit, spend the extra dollars required to get a good one. Poor quality PSUs are the cause of many computer problems.

...cont'd

Has the PC crashed? Has it locked-up? Has the video system failed? With no information on the screen, you have no clues as to what's going on.

So what can be done in this situation? Well, the first thing you can try is exercising some patience. While your system could well be screwed up, it may respond if you simply give it time, say a couple of minutes.

If not, look for a Suspend or Hibernate key. Some keyboards have designated keys for these functions (particularly laptops), which you may not have noticed. If you do find one, it may just do the trick.

Failing that, you will have no option but to hit the PC's Reset switch to restart the PC. Once back in Windows, you then need to investigate the issue to prevent a recurrence.

The most common cause of this problem is outdated or incompatible hardware drivers – video and audio cards in particular. Visit the manufacturer's website of any recently added hardware device and download/install the most recent driver for it.

Then uninstall any recently added software. Incompatible third-party software can interfere with power management – video and audio related applications being prime candidates.

Peripherals, such as SCSI adapters, modems, and CD/DVD drives all contain chips that are preloaded with relevant instructions (known as firmware). If you have recently added one of these, see if a firmware update is available from the manufacturer. Also check if a BIOS update is available from the motherboard's manufacturer. Note that if you are running Windows 7, the BIOS must comply with the ACPI 2.0 specification.

Make sure your hard drive has enough free space. When ACPI is initiated, it creates a snapshot of the system's state on the hard drive. When the user wants the PC back, the data in the snapshot is used to restore the system. This snapshot is equal in size to the amount of memory installed in the PC.

So if you have 4 GB of memory, the snapshot will require 4 GB of hard drive space. Problems can arise if the amount available is close to this figure.

Hot tip

If your system is relatively modern, it should have a Windows utility that will enable you to update your BIOS quickly and easily.

Drive Fragmentation

If the PC simply takes an abnormal length of time to come out of power management mode, the cause could well be a severely fragmented hard drive. In this situation, the data that comprises the saved snapshot will be scattered randomly across the drive's storage disks and so the drive's read/write heads will take a long time to rebuild it. While this is happening, the monitor will remain stubbornly blank. Running Windows defragmenting utility will soon fix this.

Of course, if you don't want the bother of finding the cause of this issue, the quickest way to eliminate it is to simply disable ACPI. You can do this as follows:

1 Go to Start, Control Panel, Power Options. Click Change plan settings

2 From the "Put the computer to sleep:" drop-down list, select Never. Then click Save changes

Hot tip

Windows users will find the disk defragmenting utility by going to Start, All Programs, Accessories, System Tools.

Hot tip

If you are using a laptop, power management is important, so we recommend that you take the trouble to resolve any related issues that may arise. For users of desktop PCs, it may not be worth bothering with.

Display is Scrambled

This is a fault that is unlikely to occur out of the blue. Usually, it is the result of the user (or someone else) fiddling with the display's resolution or refresh rate settings.

When either of these are set to a figure that the monitor is not capable of displaying, the screen will become scrambled, as shown above. As there is nothing intelligible on the screen, there is no way of reverting to a setting that works. The solution is to restart the PC, boot into Safe Mode and when back in Windows, do the following:

Right-click on the desktop and click Screen Resolution. From the Resolution drop-down list, select a lower setting and reboot.

If the display is still scrambled, reboot into Safe Mode again, go to Screen Resolution as shown above but this time click Advanced settings and select the Monitor tab in the new dialog box. Check the "Hide modes that this monitor cannot display" checkbox and then from the Monitor Settings drop-down list, select the highest available refresh rate. Then reboot.

This should resolve the issue. If it doesn't, you almost certainly have a faulty power supply unit.

Hot tip

A monitor's refresh rate is the number of times the video system draws (refreshes) a picture on the screen in one second. Thus, the higher the rate the sharper the picture appears to the user.

Hot tip

A monitor's resolution refers to the number of pixels used to display an image. The higher the resolution, the more pixels are used and thus the sharper the picture. However, if the resolution being used requires a higher pixel count than the monitor can physically display, the screen will become garbled.

Screen Colors Are Wrong

It's very rare to see a computer monitor that displays colors as they actually are. This is because most users are not fussy about this issue and are content as long as they look about right.

However, there are some applications where screen colors need to be accurate. High-end graphics applications are obvious examples but these aren't relevant to the average user. One that is though, is when a color mismatch exists between a printer's output and what is viewed on the monitor. It can be extremely irritating when a lot of time and effort has been expended in tweaking the color, brilliance and contrast of, say, holiday snaps only for them to look somewhat different when printed.

It could be, of course, that the printer settings are wrong rather than the monitor's but usually it is the latter that needs correcting, so this is the one to start with. The first thing to check is the monitor's display mode. All modern monitors provide several of these, e.g. Movie, Photo, Standard, etc, and they will be found on the monitor's setup menu. Cycle through these to see if a particular mode is better than the one currently in use.

The next step is to calibrate your monitor. This is a very simple exercise that can be done with the aid of a calibration utility. If you are running Windows 7, you have one right at hand. If not though, you may well find one on your monitor's installation disk or available for download from the manufacturer's website.

Use the Windows 7 calibration utility as follows:

1 Go to Start, Control Panel, Display. At the left-hand side of the dialog box, click Calibrate Color

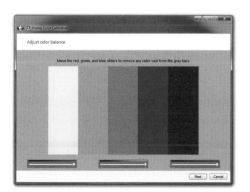

2 Follow the prompts to calibrate the monitor's color, gamma, contrast and brilliance

Hot tip

Once you have got your monitor to display color accurately, you need to configure your printer to work from the same color settings – see page 129.

Hot tip

You should also check your monitor's color setting. Do this by right-clicking on the desktop and selecting Screen resolution. In the dialog box that opens, click Advanced settings and then click the Monitor tab. Under Colors, make sure the color setting is set to True Color (32 bit).

...cont'd

If you are not happy with the results of the calibration, or would rather do the adjustments manually, the video system's software will provide you with the required adjustment options. Below we see ATI's Catalyst Control Center – this offers a large range of graphic settings, e.g. color vibrance, saturation, tint, etc.

Hot tip

If you don't have a monitor calibration utility, there are plenty available for free on the Internet. There are also many sites that offer online calibration.

Display is Distorted

Display distortion takes many forms: splodges of color, too much of one color, unwanted artifacts, banding etc. A typical example is shown right.

This type of display fault has many causes. One of the most likely is a corrupt video driver so eliminate this first by reinstalling it as described previously.

Another good candidate is a loose connection between the video output and the monitor – make sure both ends of the video cable are securely connected. The cable itself could be damaged – check this out by replacing it.

An overheating component (typically the PSU, CPU, video card or memory) can also be the cause of this issue. Open up the case and check that the case, PSU, CPU and video card fans are all operational. If any are not, replace them. While you have the case open, remove all the dust from the circuit boards and the case's air intake grilles. If the problem persists, replace the video card.

Display is Very Slow

When a graphic (image) is loaded, such as the Windows startup screen, it does not appear instantly. Instead, you can literally see it being drawn on the screen by the video system. This is quite a common problem and is the result of the video driver having been uninstalled (intentionally or otherwise) or having become corrupted. In this situation Windows takes over and installs a basic VGA video driver, which will work with all setups.

However, while it will provide a picture, it will be slow. Check this out as follows:

1 Right-click the desktop and select Screen resolution. In the dialog box that opens, click Advanced settings

2 If there is nothing listed under Adapter Type then your video driver is either missing or is corrupt

3 Place the video system's installation disk in the CD/DVD drive. Then click the Properties button in the Adapter dialog box, click the Driver tab and then click Update Driver. This opens the Driver Update wizard. Select the first option "Search automatically for updated driver software", and Windows will find and install the driver

Hot tip

Another way of checking your video driver is by looking in the Device Manager. Details of the driver currently installed will be found under "Display adapter".

Hot tip

Selecting the first option offered by the Driver Update wizard is recommended as it will also search online. If it finds a driver that is more recent than the one on the disk, that's the one it will install.

No Sound

Your computer is not talking to you. The first thing to establish is whether the problem applies to the whole system or just to parts of it. Do this as follows:

1 Go to Start, Control Panel, Sound. Click the Sounds tab

2 Select a sound file – any one will do

Hot tip

If the problem occurs after upgrading your system to a more modern operating system, there is a good possibility that your sound system is not compatible with it. You may need to download an updated driver from the manufacturer's website to get it working.

3 Click Test

If the selected file plays OK then the problem is not too serious as it indicates that the sound system, speakers and speaker connections are all OK. The problem will be specific to a particular application. Reinstalling the application in question will usually fix the problem.

If, however, it doesn't then you need to investigate further.

Checking the Sound System

The next thing to check is that you actually have a sound system.

1 Go to Start, Control Panel, Sound. Then click the Playback and Recording tabs

Hot tip

System Restore (see page 38) is another method of restoring a corrupt sound driver.

2 If there is nothing listed under the Playback and Recording tabs then the driver is missing or corrupt

3 Reinstall the driver to restore the sound

Checking the Speakers

If the sound driver checks out then the problem will be with the speakers, the speaker connections or the volume controls.

Hot tip

Make sure the sound system's Mute option has not been enabled in error.

Make sure that the speakers are connected to the system correctly as described on page 65. If your system has a sound card, be sure to check that the speakers are connected to this rather than to the integrated motherboard sound system.

If your speakers are of the powered type, check that they are receiving power. Finally, check the volume controls, both on the speakers (if they have one) and on the PC.

Intermittent Sound

Your computer's sound is skipping. As with display distortion, the most common cause of this is a corrupt driver; reinstalling the sound system's driver will usually resolve the issue.

If not, the problem could be with the speakers or their connections. Check the speaker jacks are pushed in all the way and then check the speakers themselves by connecting a different set.

You may also experience this problem if you ask your computer to do more than it is capable of. While this is unlikely with a modern or well specified system, if yours is approaching, or past, its sell-by date simply running too many applications simultaneously may overload the memory with resulting sound issues. Closing some of the applications may be all that's needed.

On a related note, if you have recently added, or upgraded, a hardware device, the system resources required by the new device may have the same effect. In both these scenarios, installing more memory will usually effect a permanent fix.

Electrical Interference

The most common type of interference is that produced by nearby electrical devices – this manifests itself in the form of crackling, humming or popping sounds. If the problem has appeared out of the blue, this will be almost certainly be the cause. See if anything unusual has been placed in the vicinity of the PC. If not, take a look outside – it may be some workmen operating a generator on the street.

If it happens after installing a sound card in the PC, it could be another component in the PC that is causing the interference. Try moving the card to a position where it is as far away from other components as possible. Also, make sure there are no cables in contact with each other.

Motherboard integrated sound systems are well known for this issue. If you have just installed a new motherboard and are experiencing interference, the only solution other then replacing the motherboard, is to disable the on-board sound and install a separate sound card.

Hot tip

If your sound hisses and crackles, the cause will be electrical interference from nearby power sources.

7 Multimedia

In this chapter, we look at one of the most popular uses of a PC – multimedia. Related applications include video, gaming and images.

Movies Won't Play

You want to watch a video on your PC but it just won't play. You may get an error message or nothing happens at all. Why?

The answer depends to a great extent on what type of video you are trying to play. We'll start with the most problematic of all the various types of video – commercial movies.

Decoding Software

Commercial movies are currently coded in two formats – DVD and Blu-ray. To play either on a computer, relevant decoding software must be installed on the PC. If it is not, you will get an error message. For example: "Windows Media Player cannot play the DVD because a compatible DVD decoder is not installed on your computer."

If you get an error message of this type, the solution is simple – install the required decoding software. Virtually all decoding software also provides a media player; a good example being Cyberlink's PowerDVD.

However, these programs all cost money: an alternative that is free is a media player called VLC. This can be downloaded from www.videolan.org and will play DVD and Blu-ray movies. It is also an extremely good media player in general and is a recommended download.

Hot tip

Windows Media Player (WMP), included in Windows Vista Home Premium and Windows Vista Ultimate, will play DVDs but not Blu-ray. The version of WMP included with Windows 7 Home Premium, Professional, Ultimate, and Enterprise, will play both DVDs and Blu-ray. Previous versions of Windows cannot play either.

84

Blu-ray movie playing on VLC media player

Copyright Protection

Film studios spend millions of dollars to produce a movie and so get extremely upset at the thought of people watching a pirated copy for nothing. In an effort to prevent this, they employ various techniques that make it impossible to play a copied disc.

When a user attempts to play such a disc, an error message, as shown right, will pop up.

The bottom line is that this is a movie the user is simply not going to be able to watch.

Various types of protection are used with DVD movies but the most common is called CSS (Content Scrambling System). With this technique, an encrypted key is placed on a part of the disc that is unaccessible to the user, i.e. it cannot be copied to another disc. The manufacturers' of DVD players are provided with a CSS decryption module (under licence), which they build into their devices in the form of a chip. The firmware contained in the chip is able to recognize and decrypt the key in a legitimate disc.

Blu-ray movies are copy protected with a similar technique known as AACS (Advanced Access Content System).

An unfortunate aspect of CSS and AACS is that things can go wrong. Internet forums are awash with tales from disgruntled users who are unable to get their legally acquired movies to play. This happens for two reasons: One, the DVD drive's firmware (which cannot be updated) can become corrupt thus rendering the device useless as far as playing copy protected discs is concerned. Second, on old DVD drives, the CSS decryption module may be out-of-date and thus won't be able to decrypt current DVD movies. They may not even have a decryption module at all.

However, the former issue has been addressed with the introduction of Blu-ray. This format also employs a separate technique called BD+, that can execute code included on discs to verify, authorize, revoke, and automatically update players should the need arise.

...cont'd

Another form of copy protection, known as High Bandwidth Digital Content Protection (HDCP), can be the cause of movies not playing even though the disc is legally acquired and the drive is capable of decoding the encrypted key.

Rather than copy protecting the data on the disc, HDCP copy protects the hardware used to play it. It works by encrypting a digital signal with a key that requires authentication from both the transmitting and receiving device. If authentication fails then the signal fails, which means no picture on the monitor.

Therefore, both the video system (transmitter) and the monitor (receiver) have to be HDCP compliant. If either is not you will get an error message like the one shown below:

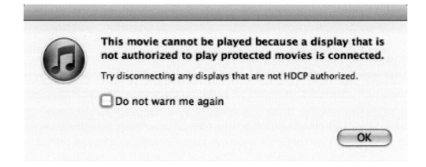

This movie cannot be played because a display that is not authorized to play protected movies is connected.

Try disconnecting any displays that are not HDCP authorized.

☐ Do not warn me again

OK

 Don't forget

Your monitor must be connected to the video system via either a DVI or HDMI cable in order to play high definition movies.

Furthermore, the cable used to connect the video system to the monitor has to use digital technology, e.g. DVI or HDMI. If a VGA cable (which is analog) is used, the movie will play but not in high-definition.

While most modern video cards, and integrated video systems in recent high-end motherboards, are HDCP compliant, the same cannot be said for monitors. Therefore, anyone thinking of using anything other than a very up-to-date PC to watch high-definition commercial movies, will almost certainly have some upgrading to do. Even if the PC itself is OK, it may well be that the monitor needs to replaced by a HDCP compliant model.

In the case of DVD movies, they also need to be sure that their DVD drive can handle CSS copy protection, i.e that it is not one of those sold without a CSS decryption module, or one that is out-of-date.

Codecs

Moving on from movies to more general types of video, e.g. clips downloaded from the Internet, refusal to play is usually the result of the required software not being available on the PC. When this happens, your media player may play a visualization as shown below. Alternatively, depending on the player, you may get an error message stating that a codec is missing.

Visualizations are very pretty but you'd rather see your movie

Hot tip

Codecs are used for both video and sound, so you may have a situation in which your movie plays but without any sound. The solution is the same – identify the missing sound codec and download it from the Internet.

Both of these indicate that the media player hasn't been able to find the correct codec. Codecs are small software programs that are used to compress a video or sound file when it is created in order to reduce the file size. When the file is played it is decompressed and to do that the codec that compressed it must be on the computer.

The most used type of video codec is AVI (Audio-Video Interleaved) of which there are many versions. The two most common are called DIVX and XVID. If you get the above problem, you should download and install both of these codecs as it's very likely that the file has been compressed with one or the other. You can find them at www.divxmovies.com.

However, there are many different types of codec and so it may be that your movie or sound file still won't play. In this situation, you need to know the codec used by the file. Go to www.headbands. com/gspot and download a program called Gspot. Open the video file in Gspot and you will be able to see the codec used to compress it. Then do an Internet search for it.

Hot tip

If you've downloaded the VLC media player as per our advice on page 84, this program will also specify the codec used by a media file. On the menu bar, click Tools and then Codec Information.

Video Playback is Poor

Your videos are jerky or flicker, or you see lines on the screen.

These problems are often the result of an underpowered system and will be most noticeable when playing movies from a Blu-ray disc. Good Blu-ray playback will require a CPU running at a speed of at least 2.5 GHz and, ideally, it should be a dual- or quad-core model. In terms of memory, 1 GB of system memory and 256 MB of video memory is the minimum needed.

Note that for DVD playback, system hardware is not an issue unless you have a really old PC.

A damaged, or outdated, video driver can also cause these problems. Look for a more recent version or reinstall the existing one. If the video is a Windows Media Video (WMV) file, make sure DirectX video acceleration is enabled as described below:

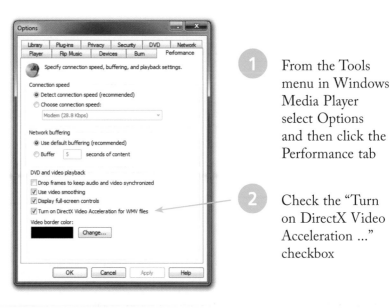

 From the Tools menu in Windows Media Player select Options and then click the Performance tab

Check the "Turn on DirectX Video Acceleration ..." checkbox

If playback is still poor then you probably have a codec problem. First, the codec used by the video file may be damaged. Establish what the codec is with a program such as Gspot and then download/install a copy from the Internet.

Second, have you installed one of the various codec packs available on the Internet? Incompatibilities are known to exist with some of the components in these packs, which can cause playback problems. If you have, uninstall it.

Games don't Play Well

We'll start with the worst problem you can have – when a game simply refuses to run at all. If you have had the game running previously without problems, sudden refusal to play will be the result of a change you have recently made to your system. The one most likely change to cause this problem is upgrading to a new operating system. In this situation, the game will probably be several years old and thus simply incompatible with the new OS.

There are two ways to fix this. First, go to the game manufacturer's website and see if there is an update (patch) available to make the game compatible. If not, the second method is to use Windows Compatibility mode to recreate the operating system environment that the game was designed to use. We explain how to do this on pages 61-62.

If the problem is poor performance, e.g. game play is slow, stutters, freezes, crashes the PC, images are blocky, etc; the cause is almost certainly an under-powered system. It is a fact that of all the applications that can be run on a PC, 3D games can be the most demanding in terms of hardware requirements.

Before you do anything though, are you using a video system integrated in the motherboard? If you are (particularly if the PC is several years old), this is almost certainly why your games don't play well. Integrated video, no matter how recent it may be, will never provide a level of game play to match that of a dedicated video card. If this is the case, you may need to buy a video card.

If you already have a video card, the first thing to check is the game's recommended system requirements, which will be listed on the box and in the documentation. Then see if your system is up to the required specifications. If not, you may have to upgrade it. Before you do, though, try a few simple steps that can sometimes free up enough resources to make the game playable:

- Switch off and then restart the PC. This will clear the memory – see margin note

- Make sure no other applications are running

- Set up Windows for best performance as opposed to best appearance. We describe how to do this on page 54

Hot tip

Closing an application doesn't necessarily mean it will release the memory it was using. Sometimes programs will leave fragments of themselves behind. The only way to clear the memory completely is to switch off the PC as it will retain data as long as it is powered up.

...cont'd

Next, visit the website of your video card manufacturer and download the latest driver for the card.

Then make sure your system is using the latest version of DirectX. DirectX is a technology developed by Microsoft that facilitates the displaying of multimedia elements such as full color graphics, video, and 3D animation.

The majority of modern games are written around this technology and require a specific version of DirectX to be installed on the computer. Check it out as follows:

Hot tip

DirectX is a set of Application Program Interfaces (APIs) developed by Microsoft to enable programmers to write software that accesses hardware features of a computer without knowing exactly what hardware will be installed on the machine. DirectX achieves this by creating an intermediate layer that translates generic hardware commands into specific commands for particular items of hardware.

1 Click Start and in the Search box, type dxdiag and then press Enter

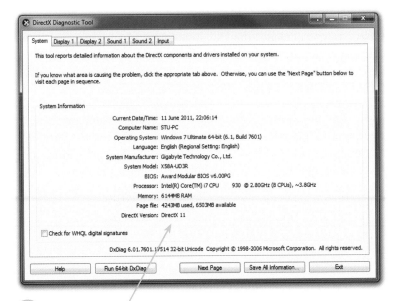

2 Here you see the version of DirectX installed on your PC

If the installed version is older than the one specified in the game's requirements, go to Microsoft's website, and download and install the latest version.

If you are still unable to get your game running smoothly, your last option before having to upgrade your system's hardware, is to tweak the game's settings.

Try the following:

1) If you haven't already done so, reinstall the game and choose the option that installs the majority (or all) of the game's data on the hard drive. The less the game has to access the CD/DVD drive, the more smoothly it will run

2) Try reducing the amount of action, e.g. reduce the number of opponents in a battle, cars in a racing game, etc. The less that is going on, the less being asked of the PC

3) Go into the game's graphics setup options and reduce the screen resolution. Then reduce settings such as Anti-Aliasing, Shadows, and Textures. These features improve graphic quality considerably but do place a heavy load on the PC

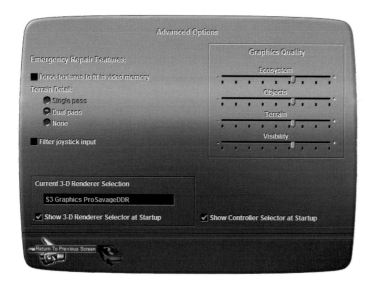

Graphics options for a PC game. Lowering the graphics quality will speed up game play

If you've got as far as this, it's time to acknowledge that you are never going to have an acceptable level of game play with your existing setup. Get your wallet out and upgrade your system.

Hot tip

Before buying any 3D game, make sure your CPU and memory match its recommended system requirements. These will be somewhere on the box.

Don't forget

Achieving a smooth level of game play is usually a compromise between graphics quality and performance, and will require a certain amount of trial and error.

Hot tip

If the game's installation options allow you to install the entire game to the hard drive, do so. Having to constantly retrieve data from the CD/DVD drive can cause the game to stutter.

Photo Editing Tips

Calibrate the Monitor

The first thing you must do is calibrate your monitor. If it is incorrectly set up then no matter how carefully you edit your images, when you print, or view them on a different monitor, they will look different.

Users of Windows 7 can use the calibration utility included with this operating system – see pages 77-78. Alternatively, one may be provided on your monitor's installation disk. If not, download a suitable application from the Internet.

Convert the Image to a Lossless Format

Image formats are either lossy or lossless. Every time a lossy image is edited, some loss of image data occurs. Thus, the more times it is edited, the worse the end result. Lossless images, on the other hand, can be edited any number of times with no loss of quality.

So before you edit any image of a lossy type, e.g. JPEG, convert it to either a TIFF or a PNG format, both of which are lossless. Having edited the image, convert it back to the original file type. This ensures that the original image quality is retained.

Brightness and Contrast Adjustments

All image editors provide brightness and contrast controls, and often a one-click setting that does the job automatically. While these can work well, sometimes the result is less than optimal.

A more accurate way is to use the image editor's Histogram control (shown below). This gives a graphical representation of the image, showing its color distribution in terms of brightness and darkness. The left of the graph represents black and the right represents white. Consider the under-exposed picture shown below:

Hot tip

If you have an image that cannot be replaced, make a copy and use that for editing. If you mess it up, you've still got the original.

Hot tip

The JPEG format, which is commonly used by digital cameras, is a lossy format.

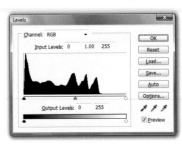

The histogram of the image shows that its data is over to the left of the graph, i.e. its dark tones are overemphasized (if an image's exposure is correct, the data will be centered in the graph).

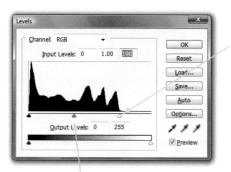

1 Drag the white pointer to where the data begins. This sets the image's brightness to the correct level

2 Now adjust the gray pointer in the middle to set the image's mid-tone contrast

Color Correction

The next adjustment you might need to make is to the image's colors. If it has too much of one color, i.e. a color cast, correct it with the Color Balance control.

If all the colors are wrong, i.e. are under- or over-emphasized, correct them with the Saturation control (part of the Hue/Saturation control as shown below).

If just one color is wrong, select the color from the Hue/Saturation control's Edit menu and then adjust it with the Saturation control. Adjustments will affect that color only – see next page.

Hot tip

Another way to adjust the color of a specific area of an image is to select the area with a selection tool such as the Marquee or Lasso tool. Any changes you make will affect the selected area only.

94

In this image, the grass and trees have a yellowish tint that gives a slightly washed-out or faded look

Adjusting the green channel only gives the grass and trees a more natural color, while the other colors remain unchanged

Sharpening

The first rule of image sharpening is that this process should be the last edit to be made. The second rule is to ignore the Sharpen and Sharpen More tools, as they provide little user control and usually result in the image being sharpened incorrectly (usually over sharpened).

The tool you should use is the Unsharp Mask. When using this, you need to zoom in closely so that you can work with precision.

Many imaging programs provide a zoom-in preview window for this purpose. If yours doesn't, use the program's zoom control to get in close.

Beware

Sharpening tools should be used with restraint. Overuse of them will ruin your images.

The rule of thumb is to look for halos along sharp edges. When you see these, reduce the Threshold setting until the halos disappear. Then you should be about right.

8 The Internet

This chapter looks at problems experienced when using the Internet. These include inability to access specific sites, broken and slow connections, and how to filter harmful content.

No Internet Access

You fire up your browser, specify an address and head off into cyberspace. Except you don't – all you see is a "This page cannot be displayed" error message. There are three likely reasons for this:

- The page you tried to access no longer exists
- Your Internet Service Provider (ISP) is out of service
- Your modem is misconfigured, faulty, or its connections are

The first possibility is the easiest to rule out – simply try accessing a few other sites randomly. If you cannot connect to any of them, you need to investigate further.

The next thing to check is that you are actually connected to the Internet. Hover your mouse over the Internet activity icon in the System Tray at the right-hand side of the Taskbar. You will probably see a message saying "No network access". If you do, either your ISP is out of service or there is a problem with your modem.

On the front panel of the modem, check the LED that indicates whether or not the modem is receiving data. If it's lit, this tells you that the ISP's servers are OK, and that the incoming connection to the modem is as well. If it isn't, either the ISP's servers are down, the modem is faulty or misconfigured, or you have a connection problem between the cable input to the house and the modem.

Rule out the ISP first by telephoning and asking whether there is a problem. If not, check the connection between the modem and the PC. Do this by observing the appropriate LED on the modem. If this is out, check the cable connections at both ends.

Then check that the modem is correctly installed. Open the Device Manager and, under the "Network adapters" category, make sure your modem is listed. If it isn't, the modem driver is corrupt. Reinstall it from the installation disk.

If you still can't connect, the cause will be either a faulty or misconfigured modem. The latter is the more likely with broadband modems and can occasionally cause them to lose contact with the ISP. The solution to this problem is to "power cycle" the modem – see margin note.

If this doesn't work either, you have a faulty modem – replace it.

Hot tip

If your modem is connected to an Internet device, such as a router or switch, bypass the device by connecting the modem directly to the computer.

Hot tip

If you suspect your modem is faulty, contact your ISP. They will be able to check the device from their end and tell you conclusively whether it is good or bad.

Hot tip

Power-cycle your modem by switching the PC off, disconnecting the modem and then reconnecting it before switching the PC back on. Without going into the reasons, this will clear any configuration issues that have resulted in a loss of connection.

Internet Connection is Slow

Typical problems caused by a slow connection include websites taking a long time to load, file download speeds being abnormally slow, jerky Internet media streaming, etc.

We'll start with broadband connections as these are the most common type. The first thing to establish is whether the problem is either temporary in nature, or simply out of your control. Doing this will save you wasting time and effort trying to repair something that simply can't be repaired.

Temporary Causes

There are many things that can be the cause of a temporary slow-down in your connection speed. The most common of these are:

1) Having other bandwidth-hungry applications running at the same time. Typical examples are Internet telephony such as Skype, Internet streaming such as the BBC's iPlayer, and using a peer-to-peer file sharing network

   If you can identify an open program of this nature, close it down and try again

2) Two or more computers sharing the same connection – this is quite likely if the PC is part of a network. Two PCs accessing the Internet simultaneously will each have half the available bandwidth so take one of them offline

3) Many ISPs deliberately reduce connection speeds at certain times of the day (this is never mentioned in the advertising blurb, though). There is nothing you can do about this except switch to an ISP that doesn't

4) If you are on a "capped" package, the ISP will reduce your connection speed when you have reached your allocated bandwidth allowance. If the extra cost justifies it, pay for a higher allowance, or upgrade to an uncapped package

5) A technical fault at the ISP's end. Go to the ISP's website and check its server status (or just phone them and ask)

Before you do any "fixing", be sure none of the above are causing the problem. If none of them are, you have some investigating to do.

Hot tip

All broadband providers share the available bandwidth between users. The amount an individual user gets is known as the contention ratio and, typically, for home users it will be in the region of 50:1. This means that you share the bandwidth with up to 49 other users. Business users usually have a contention ratio of 20:1.

Hot tip

You will rarely, if ever, get the maximum download speed promised by your ISP. These are headline figures for marketing purposes.

Modem Issues

The first thing to check is the modem. Obviously, it is working as you can connect but is it working properly? We mentioned before that modems can suffer from configuration issues that can break a connection. Although it is less likely, a modem configuration problem can also reduce the speed of a connection. To eliminate this possibility, power-cycle the modem as described on page 96.

Next, check that the incoming connection to the modem, and the connection from the modem to the PC, are both securely made. If necessary, also check the connection at the point where it enters the house. If you have a CATV connection that is also providing your TV with its signal, disconnect the TV so the signal is going directly to the modem.

Malware

If the problem persists then something on your PC is amiss. The most likely thing is the presence of malware. Malware is a term used to describe programs that are sneaked on to a user's PC with the intention of disruption, obtaining private information, hijacking the browser, and various other types of intrusive behavior.

These programs can slow your Internet connection speed (and, indeed, your entire computer) by an alarming degree. The most obvious indications that you have it, apart from the slowing down of your connection, or the PC, are the sudden appearance of toolbars in your browser, automatic redirection of your browser to advertising sites, sites added to your Favorites list, and a profusion of pop-up windows.

Many malware programs, though, are more subtle and present no obvious signs of their presence so if you don't experience any of the above, don't assume your PC hasn't been infected. The odds are, in fact, that it has been. As of 2010, estimates suggest that some 60 per cent of PCs worldwide have some sort of malware infection. Indeed, many PCs are found to be infected with literally hundreds of these programs.

Rule out this possible cause of your connection problems by scanning your PC with a suitable malware removal program. Two we recommend are Ad-aware (www.lavasoft.com) and Spybot Search & Destroy (www.safer-networking.org).

Don't forget

Poor cable connections can be the cause of slow connection speeds.

Hot tip

Windows 7 provides users with a built-in anti-malware utility called Windows Defender. This can be accessed via the Control Panel.

Hot tip

If you don't have a firewall, you can download a good one for free at www.zonealarm.com/security/en-us/zonealarm-pc-security-free-firewall.htm.

These are both available as free downloads and will rid your PC of unwelcome malware.

If your problem is not so much a slow connection but rather that it is simply not as fast as you think it should be, rest assured, you're not alone.

ISPs are well known for highlighting the maximum possible speed available in their various packages and then delivering something that is considerably less. You can check what your real-world connection speed is by going to a speed test website. A typical example is shown below:

This shows the author's connection speed as being 9.86 Mbps. (This particular package is advertised with a claimed maximum speed of 20 Mbps!)

Hot tip

No malware removal program is perfect so we suggest you don't rely on just one to keep your PC secure. Scan your system with two or even three malware removal programs.

Hot tip

When doing a broadband speed test site, use one that is situated as near to your location as possible.

Websites/Pages are Inaccessible

There are a number of reasons why you may not be able to access a certain website or web page. The following are the most common.

Site Congestion

Popular sites, such as the Microsoft site for example, can at times become extremely congested with thousands of users all trying to access them simultaneously. If it can't load the site, your browser will eventually give up and display a "Page cannot be displayed" error message. The only thing you can do in this situation is to try again later.

Cookies

If you are unable to access a specific page within a website, the usual reason is that your browser is configured to not accept cookies – see top margin note. Be aware that some sites will refuse access to a page if they are unable to place their cookie on a user's PC – a typical example of when they may do this is accessing password-protected pages.

Check this out as follows:

Hot tip

Cookies are small text files that websites download to users' PCs. They are used to track user activity on a website and to store user information and preferences. This allows sites to show customized pages when a user revisits the site.

Hot tip

While the vast majority of cookies are harmless, some can be used to access information on PCs. For this reason, many users disable cookies.

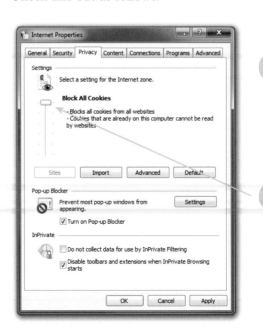

1 Open Internet Options in the Control Panel and click the Privacy tab

2 Make sure the slider is not set to Block All Cookies. If it is, then drag it down a level

On a related note, many web pages contain embedded controls or programs. When you click the link, the program or control should run. However, it will only do so if you have the program installed on your PC.

Typical examples of this are Adobe Flash Player, which is used by many sites to display video; and Java, a common use of which is for the calendars found on travel booking sites. If you don't have the program in question installed, you will usually get a message saying which one is required, and a link to a website from which you can download it.

Firewalls

A firewall is a program that prevents people accessing the computers of other users via the Internet – an activity commonly known as hacking.

Unfortunately, firewalls can sometimes do the opposite, i.e. prevent a user from accessing websites. So, if you are having access problems and have a firewall installed, try disabling it.

Assuming you are using the firewall provided by Windows 7, do this as follows:

1 Go to Start, Control Panel, Windows Firewall. At the left, click "Turn Windows Firewall on or off". In the new dialog box, check "Turn off Windows Firewall..."

If this resolves the issue then you may need to reconfigure the firewall's settings to prevent a recurrence. We don't have space to describe this procedure here but you will find many websites that provide full instructions.

Get Rid of Browser Pop-Up Windows

Hot tip

Pop-ups can be useful so most pop-up blockers allow the user to accept pop-ups from specified sites and block them from others.

Hot tip

Not all pop-up blockers are created equal. Some block all pop-ups while others are more "intelligent" and allow legitimate content to be displayed.

Hot tip

Most pop-up blockers provide a manual override key (usually the CTRL key). Hold the key down when you click the link and any pop-ups associated with the link will be allowed.

If used for the right purpose, such as displaying useful information, pop-up windows are an acceptable part of browsing the Internet. Unfortunately, however, they are all too often used to display irritating advertisements and other such stuff.

The solution to this problem is to use a pop-up blocker. These programs automatically prevent a website opening pop-up windows in your browser.

Users of Windows 7 and Vista have a built-in pop-up blocker. However, if you are using Windows XP or an earlier Windows version, you will either have to install Internet Explorer 9 (a free download from www.microsoft.com), or install a third-party pop-up blocker.

A quick search of the Internet will reveal dozens of these, some good, some not so good.

One that we recommend comes with the Google Toolbar (a useful browser add-on in itself). Download this from http://toolbar.google.com.

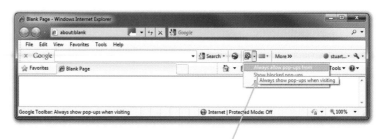

The Google pop-up blocker

Another option is to download and install a third-party browser. For example, the Firefox browser (available free from www.mozilla.com) comes with a built-in pop-up blocker.

Quite apart from this, Firefox is in any case generally considered to be a superior browser to Internet Explorer.

Where Did My Downloaded File Go?

You've downloaded a file from the Internet but you can't find it on your PC.

If you are running Internet Explorer 8, by default the downloaded file will be saved in the Download folder in your user profile folder. This can be accessed by clicking the Start button and then your profile folder at the top-right of the Start menu.

However, you may have selected a different location in the "Save" dialog box and then forgotten it. Alternatively, you may have selected a different location inadvertently. You may also be using a third-party browser which has a different default download location.

In any of these scenarios, you will have no idea where the file is. However, virtually all browsers will "remember" the last user specified download location and use this for all subsequent downloads. This makes it very simple to locate a downloaded file you have lost.

1 Open your browser and go to any site that offers a file for download. Click the file's download link

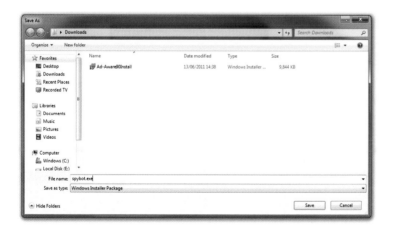

Hot tip

Third-party browsers often have a different default download folder from that of Internet Explorer. You will be able to see which it is (and also change it) from Options on the browser's Tools menu.

Hot tip

All browsers will, by default, save a download in the location used for the previous download.

In the "Save" dialog box, you will see the previously downloaded file, plus the name of the folder it is saved in.

Quick Internet Searching

Search engines certainly speed up the process of finding something specific on the Internet. However, simply typing in a relevant word and clicking Go is not the most efficient way to use them.

For example: type the word "tiger" in Google and you will get millions of pages to look through. These will range from the Tiger Lily restaurant in Shanghai and Tiger Woods the golfer to, not surprisingly, pages about tigers. Finding something specific can take a long time.

So, to help users narrow their searches, all the major search engines offer an Advanced Search. This will offer various options, such as language-specific searches, searches restricted to pages updated within a specific time-frame, etc.

However, before you try these, the following simple search aids may be all you need.

Phrase Searches
By enclosing your keywords in quotation marks, you will do a phrase search. This will return pages with all the keywords in the order entered. For example, "atlanta falcons" will return pages mainly concerning the Atlanta NFL team. Most pages regarding Atlanta (the city) or falcons (the birds) will be excluded.

The - Operator

The - operator allows you to exclude words from a search. For example, if you are looking for windows (glass ones), type: windows -microsoft -7 -vista -xp -me -98 -2000

This will eliminate millions of pages devoted to the various Windows operating systems.

The + Operator

Most search engines exclude common words such as "and" and "to", and certain single digits and letters. If you want to make sure a common word is included in the search, type + before it.

For example: world war +1 (make sure there is a space between the + and the previous word).

The OR Operator

The OR operator allows you to search for pages that contain word A OR word B OR word C, etc. For example, to do a search on camping trips in either Yosemite or Yellowstone national parks, you would type the following: "camping trips" yosemite OR yellowstone

Combinations of Operators

To narrow your searches further, you can use combinations of search operators and phrase searches. Using our Atlanta Falcons example, typing "atlanta falcons" +nfl -"olympic games" -"birds of prey" will return a far higher proportion of relevant pages.

Numrange Searches

Numrange searches can be used to ensure that search results contain numbers within a specified range. You can conduct a numrange search by specifying two numbers, separated by two periods with no spaces.

For example, you would search for computers in the $600 to $900 price bracket by typing: computers $600..900.

Numrange can be used for all types of units.

Hot tip

The most useful operators are: - (NOT) and quotation marks (phrase searching). These two operators can whittle a search result that would otherwise be several million pages down to a few hundred.

Repair Internet Explorer

Internet Explorer is a highly complex piece of software and, as with Windows itself, it can over time become corrupted to the extent that it no longer works properly or little niggles and errors creep in.

If you are experiencing problems when using Internet Explorer, try the following:

Internet Explorer Add-Ons

While browser add-ons can enhance your browsing, they do sometimes conflict with other software on your computer. To eliminate these as a possible source of the problem, try running Internet Explorer without any add-ons.

Do it by going to Start, All Programs, Accessories, System Tools, Internet Explorer (No Add-ons).

If this resolves the problem, start Internet Explorer in the usual way (add-ons enabled) and then on the menu bar click Tools, Manage add-ons. Then disable them one by one until the offender has been identified.

Reset Internet Explorer

If disabling add-ons doesn't solve the problem, try resetting Internet Explorer back to its default settings.

Hot tip

If Internet Explorer repeatedly stops responding, do the following:

- Scan the PC for malware

- Clear the contents of the Temporary Internet Files folder

Hot tip

Resetting Internet Explorer removes all changes that have been made to its settings since the time of its installation. It does not delete your Favorites and Feeds, though.

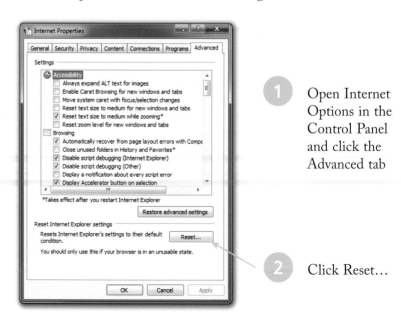

1 Open Internet Options in the Control Panel and click the Advanced tab

2 Click Reset...

Protect the Kids

The Internet is a minefield that can expose gullible and trusting kids to many different types of threat. All responsible parents will want to minimize, if not eliminate completely, the risks their children are exposed to.

There are many commercially available programs available that help them to do this, such as Net Nanny, CyberPatrol, Norton Parental Controls, etc. The best of these applications enable parents to control and monitor literally every aspect of what the typical child might want to do on a computer and the Internet.

However, this is a Windows related book so we will look at what this operating system has to offer in the way of child protection. We'll start with Windows 7's in-built utility - Parental Controls.

Go to Start, Control Panel, Parental Controls. In the dialog box that opens, you will be prompted to set up a user account for each child you want to protect.

Hot tip

By itself, the Parental Controls utility does not offer much to get excited about. However, when used in conjunction with the Live Family Safety utility (see next page), you can control pretty much anything your kids do, not only on the Internet but also on the PC itself.

107

Having created a new account, click its icon to open the settings dialog box. Here, you will be able to set parameters such as time limits, game ratings, and which programs can be used.

However, this application doesn't allow you to control which websites your children can access nor does it provide a monitoring facility. To do these, and others, you need to fire up your browser and head to www.download.live.com. Download and install the Family Safety utility.

Don't forget

A big advantage of the Live Family Safety utility is that it is web based. This means you can monitor and control your children's Internet activities even when you are away from home.

This program provides a web based control panel (shown above) from which you can do the following:

- Block/allow specific websites

- Use web filtering to block unsuitable content. Different filters can be created for each child

- Block file downloads

- Control and monitor who your kids are communicating with via instant messaging software, such as Windows Messenger, and email

- Get monitoring reports on what your kids have been doing both on the Internet and the PC

- Access and adjust each child's safety settings from the Family Safety website, accessible from any PC

Used in conjunction, the Parental Control and Family Safety utilities not only enable parents to control everything their kids do on the Internet, they also provide a degree of protection to the PC by blocking potentially dangerous downloads, and access to programs and settings on the PC.

9 Email

Email is one of the most popular and useful of all a computer's applications. It does, however, come with its own set of problems. In this chapter, we look at the most common of these.

Email Won't Send or Receive

The first thing to check is that your Internet connection is good; if not, troubleshoot as described on page 96. If your email has been working and then suddenly stops, this has to be the main suspect.

However, if you have just installed your email program, Windows itself or a program downloaded from the Internet, or the PC has just crashed; misconfigured email settings are the most likely explanation.

Having established that your Internet connection is good, switch the PC off and then back on. This can often repair configuration issues.

If the problem persists, check out your anti-virus program (assuming you are running one). These programs check all emails – incoming and outgoing – and can be the cause of transmission or reception problems. Locate the anti-virus program's Check Email function and disable it.

Your email settings are the next thing to check. The simplest way to do this is to delete your email account and then set it up again. The following shows how it's done with Windows Mail – the email program supplied with Windows Vista. Whichever email program you use though, the procedure is very similar.

Before you begin, you will need the information listed below to hand:

- The type of email server you use – POP3 (most email accounts), HTTP (services such as Hotmail), or IMAP

- The name of the incoming email server (usually POP)

- For POP3 and IMAP servers, the name of the outgoing email server (usually SMTP)

- Your account user name and password

When you've got the information, do the following:

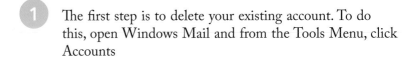

The first step is to delete your existing account. To do this, open Windows Mail and from the Tools Menu, click Accounts

Hot tip

Your account information should be available from the documentation supplied by your ISP. If it isn't, contact them and request it.

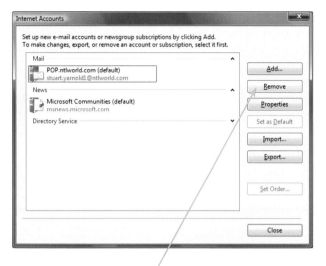

2 Select your email account and, on the right, click Remove. Then, in the same dialog box, click Add... This opens the New Account wizard

3 At the first screen, select E-mail Account

4 At the next screen, enter the name you want displayed in your outgoing messages

5 Enter your email address

Hot tip

While the setup procedure detailed here is specific to Windows Mail, the settings will be much the same whichever email application you are using. In any case, all email programs have an account setup wizard, which will help you to fill in all the required settings.

111

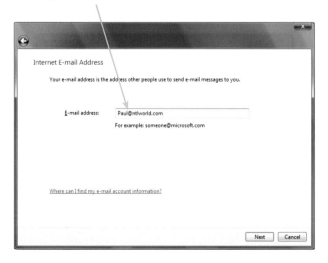

...cont'd

Hot tip

To check that your email account is working, simply send yourself an email. Alternatively, most email programs have a test facility that will check all the necessary settings, and also send and receive a test email to confirm that everything is working correctly.

6 In the Incoming and Outgoing server boxes, type POP and SMTP respectively, each followed by your ISP's address

7 At the Internet Mail Logon screen, enter your user name and password

Hot tip

Checking the "Remember password" box in the Internet Mail Logon dialog box will eliminate the need to enter it manually each time you open your email program.

Job done. You should now find that you can send and receive emails as before.

Attachments Won't Open

You click a file attached to an email you've received but it refuses to open. One cause of this is the email program's security settings. Check it out as follows:

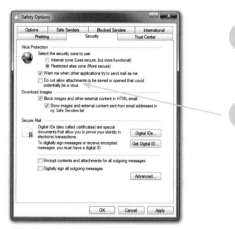

 Locate your email program's security settings

 Uncheck the option that prevents attachments from being opened

Beware

Email attachments are the most common way of transmitting viruses. This is why email programs will refuse to open an attachment that contains a file type that is potentially dangerous. You disable this protection feature at your own risk.

This issue can also be caused by not having the necessary software installed on your PC with which to open the file. For example, a spreadsheet file created with Microsoft Excel will not open unless you have Excel on your system.

In this situation, Windows will give you a "Windows cannot open this file" error message as shown right.

Select the first option (see bottom margin note), which takes you to a Microsoft website from where you may be able to identify programs compatible with the file. However, there are many sites that offer a more comprehensive list of file extensions. For example, try www. sharpened.net/extensions.

If you don't have the program on your PC, or another program that is capable of opening the file in question, you will have to acquire and install it before you will be able to open the attachment.

Hot tip

If you have a program on your PC that is capable of opening the attachment's file type, select the second option. Then browse to the program's location and select it. Windows will open the attachment with the program.

Slow Email Downloads

The larger an email, the longer it will take to receive. Text messages are just a few KB in size and download in seconds; however, messages that contain media (images, sound and video) can be much larger. Depending on what type of connection you have, these can keep your connection busy for an inordinate length of time.

With a broadband connection this probably won't be an issue, but with a dial-up connection it most definitely will be. If you don't wish to have your connection tied up for long periods, you have two options:

The first is to simply upgrade to a faster connection. The second is to create a message rule that will prevent the download of any messages over a specified size. Do this as described below:

1 Go to your email program's Message Rules. Check the "Where the message size is more than size" option, and in the next section, select "Do not download it from the server"

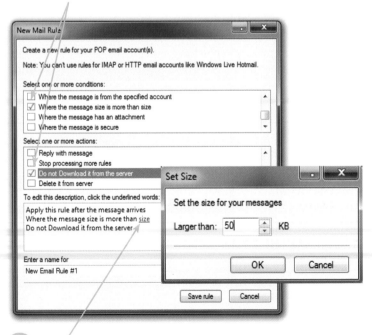

Hot tip

A maximum message size of 100 KB will block almost all emails containing media but will allow virtually all text emails to be received.

2 Under Rule Description, click "size", and in the dialog box that opens enter the maximum message size that you will accept – see bottom margin note

Images Are Too Big to Send

As anybody who regularly uses email will know, email programs allow users to insert images either directly into the email or to attach them as files.

The problem with this is that unless the image has been reduced in size in an image editor (a process that many people don't know how to do), it is possible to end up sending a huge picture file that will take the recipient ages to download.

Most people find this extremely irritating, as it can occupy their connection for a considerable length of time. So, to avoid arousing your friends' wrath use the Windows Picture Resizing utility as described below:

1 Right-click the image you want to send with your email, select Send To and then Mail Recipient

2 Select the required option – Small, Medium, Original Size, etc – and then click Attach

3 Click OK and an email message window will open with the resized image attached. All you have to do is type in the address and the message text

A couple of things to be aware of are:

- Pictures resized in this way are converted to the JPEG format, which you may or may not want

- Some image formats cannot be converted by the utility, and thus cannot be resized. Such images will be attached to the email in their original size and format

Hot tip

You can resize and attach any number of pictures simultaneously – you are not restricted to doing them one at a time.

115

Beware

Be wary of using the Small and Smaller resizing options. While these reduce the size of files enormously, they also reduce the quality of the images considerably.

Images are Missing in Emails

You receive an email that contains HTML (Internet) images but you are unable to see them. Instead, there is a white box where the images should be (with a little red X in the top-left corner), as shown below:

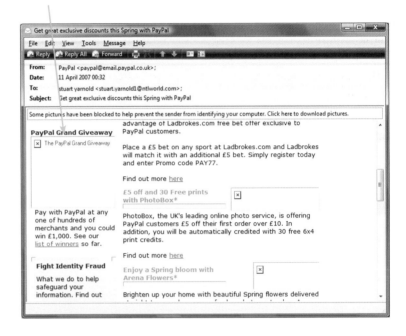

This is a security feature designed to protect users from the spammers, and from offensive images.

To reveal the images, all you have to do is click the yellow information bar above the message, or right-click on the white box and then click Download Image. However, if you would rather not have to bother with this and have the images open automatically, do the following:

 Go to your email program's security settings

 Uncheck "Block images and other external content in HTML e-mail"

Internet images will now open automatically. Before you do this, though, be sure you are aware of the possible ramifications – see margin note.

Hot tip

Images sent with spam email frequently include a snippet of hidden code known as a web beacon, which notifies the sender when the recipient has read the message. This confirms to the spammer that the email address is real and is likely to result in further junk email.

116

Emails are Missing

You open your email program and, shock, horror, there's nothing there – your emails have all vanished. Or, you may find that your emails are there but just won't open. These are both problems that many users have experienced.

To understand why this happens, you need to be aware that email programs store the user's messages in a database. Different email programs use different types of file for their database. Microsoft's Outlook, for example, uses the .pst file type, while Windows Mail uses .eml.

Unfortunately, these databases are prone to misconfiguration or corruption issues, which results in users losing their emails.

However, should this happen to you, all is not necessarily lost. If you are using Outlook Express or Outlook, both of which store email data in .pst files, there is a tool called SCANPST that, in most cases, will be able to repair your corrupt .pst file.

Hot tip

You can find out where your email database is located in the email program's Options. With Microsoft Outlook, for example, click Tools on the menu bar, then Options, Mail Setup, Data Files. Here you will see an entry specifying the name of your email database and its location.

1 Go to Start, Computer, Local Disk (C:), Program files(x86), Microsoft Office, Office 12. Scroll down until you see SCANPST

2 Click SCANPST and when the utility opens, enter the .pst file's location – see margin note. Then click Start

When the recovery procedure is finished, open your email program and your emails should now be restored. Note that SCANPST does not always work, in which case try viewing your messages with a third-party email viewer such as Mailview – see page 118.

If this doesn't work either, there is nothing else you can do other than make sure you have a backup of your emails should the problem ever happen again – see page 119.

Users of Windows Mail and Windows Live Mail can also experience the problem of lost emails, although it is less likely as the databases used by these two email clients are more robust.

However, if it does happen the recommended fix is to uninstall the program and then reinstall it. This usually resolves the issue.

If you are using Windows Live Mail, do it as follows:

1. Uninstall the program by going to Start, Control Panel, Programs and Features. Right-click Windows Live Essentials and click Uninstall

2. Then go to http://explore.live.com and click Essentials, Mail. Click the Download button and then click Run. The program will now be reinstalled

Users of Windows Mail are unable to do the above procedure as this program is integrated into Windows Vista. In this case, the only way to get a clean version is to uninstall the entire operating system and then reinstall it. For the vast majority of people, this simply won't be an option.

There are two solutions, however. The first, while not a fix as such, may enable you to view your emails. Go online and download an email viewer – these are third-party programs that can read the contents of an email database. Open the program, specify the location of the corrupt database and see if your emails are now accessible.

If not, or you want a permanent fix, the other option is to overwrite Windows Mail by downloading and installing the more recent Windows Live Mail as described above.

During the setup routine, Windows Live Mail will detect your Windows Mail installation and ask if you want to incorporate its settings and message database into the new installation – click Yes. When you run Live Mail for the first time, your emails should now be accessible.

Hot tip

A free email viewer that we recommend is Mailview. This can be downloaded from www.mitec.cz/mailview.html.

Hot tip

It is well worth upgrading to Windows Live Mail anyway as it is a better program than Windows Mail.

How to Back Up Your Emails

As we have seen on page 117, it is quite common for the databases used by email programs for the storage of messages and contacts to become corrupt or misconfigured. While it is often possible to repair these databases, sometimes it is not and the emails will be lost permanently.

Therefore, as a precaution, users should make periodic backups of their emails. We'll show you how to do this in two of the most popular email programs – Microsoft Outlook and Windows Live Mail.

Microsoft Outlook

Users of Outlook can download an email backup utility from the Microsoft website. When installed it adds a backup option to the File menu. Clicking it opens the following dialog box:

Simply specify the backup location and the frequency with which you want to be reminded to make a backup, e.g. every day, every 2 days, etc.

To restore a damaged database, open the Backup utility and click Open Backup

Windows Live Mail

If you are using Windows Live Mail, click the blue arrow at the top-left and then click Export email, Email messages.

In the next dialog box, click Microsoft Windows Live Mail. Then browse to your backup location and click Next.

Finally, click All Folders and then Next – a copy of your emails will now be saved in the specified location. To restore the database, click the blue arrow and click Import messages. Then follow the prompts.

Hot tip

If you have a particularly important message you wish to make a separate backup of, you can simply drag it out of the email program to the desired backup location. This works with all email programs.

Beware

Don't forget that any emails sent or received after you make the backup will not be included in it. So update the backup regularly to keep it current.

Dealing With Spam

If you find yourself the recipient of an endless stream of advertisements, too-good-to-be-true offers, etc, is there anything you can do to stop it?

The answer is yes and the easiest way to do it is to simply close your account and then set up a new one with a new email address – this will stop it immediately. Having done so, you then need to make sure the new account is kept out of the spammers' reach. Observing the following rules will help:

- Make your email address as long as possible

- Never post your address on a website

- If you need to give an address to access a web page, give a false one

- Never click the "Unsubscribe from this mailing list" link in a junk email. Doing this confirms your email address is real

However, it may not be practical to change your email address. In this case, you can make things difficult for the spammers with the aid of two utilities found in all email programs.

Message Rules

Message rules give the user a great deal of control over what makes it into the Inbox. For example, the table below lists just some of the options provided by Message Rules utilities:

Conditions	Actions
Specific words in the message	Delete the message
Messages from specified accounts	Do not download from the server
Messages over a specified size	Delete from the server
Messages that contain attachments	Move to a specified folder
All messages	Reply with a message

Blocked Senders List

This is a simple utility that is useful for blocking persistent emails from websites or an individual. To use it, right-click a message from the sender in question, select Junk E-mail and then "Add Sender to Blocked Senders List". Subsequent emails from the sender will automatically be placed in the Junk folder.

Beware

Chatrooms, Newsgroups and Message Boards are happy hunting grounds for spammers. Never post your email address on these sites.

Beware

Never reply to a spammer. Doing so confirms that your address is real.

Beware

Be careful when creating rules to block emails. For example, if you create a rule to delete all messages containing specific words, a legitimate message that happens to contain one of those words will also be blocked. So rather than use single words, specify phrases.

10 Peripherals

On its own, there isn't much you can do with a basic computer. Peripheral devices are essential if you want to do something useful with it. In this chapter we look mainly at the two most popular peripherals – printers and scanners – explaining the most common faults and how to fix them.

Printer doesn't Work

This is quite a common issue, which can have several causes. One of the most likely, and the easiest to remedy, is a transient configuration issue between the printer and the operating system.

This is the first thing to eliminate and all you have to do is switch the printer off, switch the PC off, switch the printer back on, and then restart the PC. Without going into the reasons, this will reset any configuration issues that may exist and will often get the printer going. If it doesn't however, the next thing to eliminate is the printer itself and this is done by printing a test page.

Printer Test Page

All printers have the facility to print a test page. Typically, this involves disconnecting the printer's interface cable (thus isolating it from the computer) and then pressing a combination of buttons – the procedure varies from printer to printer.

If the test is successful, it establishes that the printer itself is OK and that the fault is either software-related or with the connections. For instructions on how to carry out a printer test refer to your printer's documentation.

Check the Ink Levels and Nozzles

If the test page doesn't print, you have a problem with the printer. Check the following:

- Is an ink cartridge empty? Note that a warning message should pop up if this is the case. This doesn't always happen though, so check manually by clicking Start, Printers. Then click your printer's icon.

  In the menu bar of the dialog box that opens, click Printer, Properties and then the Maintenance tab. Here, you should see a View Printer Status button. Click this to open the Ink Details dialog box as shown below

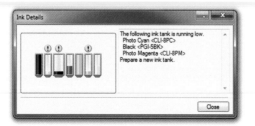

> **Hot tip**
>
> If you have replaced an ink cartridge prior to the fault manifesting itself, check you have removed the sealing tape from the cartridge.

122

> If none of the ink tanks are reported as being empty, the problem lies elsewhere

- Next, see if the ink nozzles are blocked. Do this by running the Nozzle Check utility (also on the Maintenance tab). If this indicates blocked nozzles, clear them by running the Nozzle Cleaning utility.

If this doesn't resolve the issue, you have a faulty printer

Printer Connections

Assuming the test page does print, the next thing to check is that the printer interface cable is OK and is connected to the correct port. In the case of a USB cable, try connecting it to a different USB socket.

Is The Printer Installed?

If there are no apparent problems with the printer's connections, you have a software issue. The first thing to check is that the device is installed correctly.

1 Go to Start, Devices and Printers

2 If your printer is installed, it will be listed here

If the printer isn't listed, its driver is corrupt – reinstall it.

Hot tip

If the nozzles are badly clogged, you may have to run the Cleaning utility several times to clear them.

123

...cont'd

Multiple Installations

Another common cause of a printer not working is the printer having been installed more than once. When faced with a printer issue, the first thing many people do is to reinstall it without checking to see if it actually needs to be reinstalled. When this happens, very often neither installation will work.

If this is what you've done, in the Devices and Printers dialog box, delete (right-click and click Remove Device) all but one of the installations. See if the printer works now.

If it doesn't, and you have eliminated the printer itself and its connections as the cause of the problem, and ascertained that it is correctly installed, you now know the fault is a software issue. Check the following.

Printer Settings

If the printer is listed in Devices and Printers, make sure it is configured as the default printer. This is indicated by the green check mark. If it isn't, right-click the printer's icon and select "Set As Default Printer".

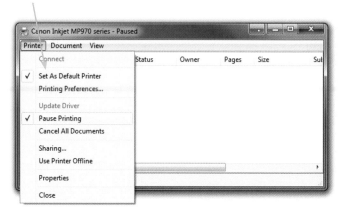

On the same menu, check that the Pause Printing option hasn't been selected inadvertently. If it has been, deselect it.

Next, check the Windows Print Manager for print jobs that aren't responding

 Open a document (any one will do) and click Print. In the Notification Area, you will now see the Print Manager icon. Click to open it

Don't forget

Check that the printer hasn't been installed more than once. This is a common mistake.

Beware

If you have more than one printing device installed on the PC, it is quite possible that one of these has set itself as the default printer.

2 Right-click on any print job that is marked as "Not Responding" and then click Cancel. This may be the document that you are currently trying to print, or an earlier document

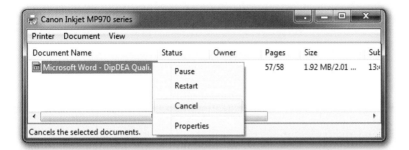

If there is one, wait until the print job has been cancelled (this can take a while). Then see if the printer is now operational.

If not, check the spool file. This is a buffer to which all print jobs are sent for queuing (this speeds up the printing process). Problems with the spool file can prevent the printer from working.

Eliminate this possibility this by opening your printer software as previously described, and clicking the Advanced tab.

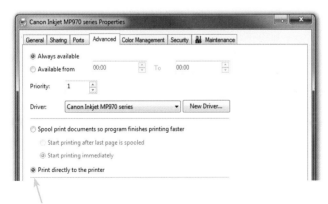

Select the "Print directly to the printer" option.

If the printer still doesn't print, uninstall it as described on page 124 and then reinstall it.

Hot tip

Check that the fault isn't being caused by the program from which you are printing – your word processor for example. This is unlikely, it must be said, but it is a possibility. Type a few lines into Notepad, for example, and see if it prints.

If it does then the program you were using originally is faulty. Close it, reopen it and try again. If the problem persists, uninstall the program and then reinstall it.

125

Printing is Slow

If a document prints at a slower than normal speed, the most likely cause is that it contains graphics (which can be enormous in size). If the computer's memory isn't large enough to cope with the volume of data being sent to it, or is already occupied by other applications, printing speed will be compromised.

If this is a one-off situation it isn't too much of a problem, but if you print many graphic-rich documents you may want to try the following:

- Decrease the size of any graphics in the document

- Increase the amount of available memory

Taking the former first, there are two ways to reduce the size of images included in a print file:

First, reduce their resolution and color depth. This is easily done with an image editor such as Irfanview, as shown below.

Second, save the image in a low-size image format such as JPEG. This can also be done in the same imaging program.

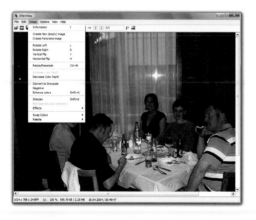

With regard to memory, you must increase the amount that is available to the printing operation.

One way to do this is to switch the PC off and then back on, which will clear its memory. Also, don't have any other programs running while printing is in progress.

If you carry out both of the above steps you should have no printing speed problems unless your machine is seriously under-specified to begin with. If this is the case, you will need to upgrade its components, memory in particular.

Hot tip

If the required print quality is not high, you can speed up printing by selecting a low-quality print setting in the printer software.

Hot tip

If you do, or plan to do, a lot of image-intensive printing and you are having problems with your existing setup, a memory upgrade will perform wonders as regards printing speed.

Print Quality is Poor

Gaps, White Horizontal Lines

These problems, and others such as faded colors, uneven color, patchy areas, etc, are usually caused by print nozzles that have become partially blocked by dried ink.

This is a result of using the printer infrequently and can be prevented by the simple expedient of printing a one page color document at least once a week.

It can also be caused by air bubbles in the nozzles. This problem is likely to occur when the user has waited until a cartridge is completely empty before replacing it, instead of doing it when the software indicates a change is needed.

Check it out by running the Nozzle Check utility. If this confirms the nozzles are blocked, clean them by running the Nozzle Cleaning utility. Both of these utilities will be found in the Utility or Maintenance tabs in the printer software.

Hot tip

Another good reason for using your inkjet printer regularly is that many printers will automatically run the Nozzle Cleaning utility after a prolonged period of inactivity. The problem with this is that the nozzle cleaning process uses a large amount of ink and, as we all know, printer ink is expensive.

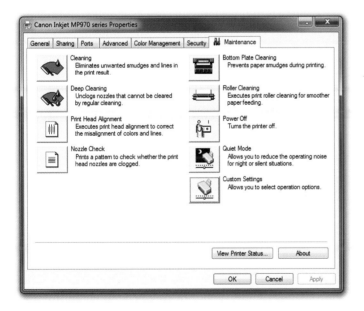

Use the Nozzle Check utility to check if the nozzles are blocked

Use the Nozzle Cleaning utility to clean the nozzles

Hot tip

Sometimes, if the nozzles are severely blocked, you will find you may need to run the Nozzle Cleaning utility several times before the print quality is up to scratch. This is yet another good reason to use the printer regularly.

...cont'd

Print Output is Smudged

The Nozzle Cleaning utility can, itself, be the cause of spoiled print output. This is because it clears the nozzles by literally forcing ink through them. While most of this ink is collected and stored in a tank, occasionally some of it escapes into the internal workings of the printer.

It's not uncommon for a printer's platen and feed rollers to become contaminated in this way. The ink will then be transferred to the document, causing streaks and smudges. If you find yourself with this problem, see if your printer software provides utilities that will clean the bottom plate and feed rollers. If not, you will have to do it manually.

Print Output is Faint

If entire documents are faint with weak colors and text; economy print resolution (also known as fast or draft) has been selected in the printer software. This print mode uses a very low resolution of about 180 dots per inch (dpi).

The solution is to select a mode that uses a higher resolution. For good quality choose the Standard mode (typically, 300 dpi), and for the best quality choose the High mode (typically, 600 dpi).

Hot tip

Ink contamination is rare with modern printers but is common with models a few years old.

128

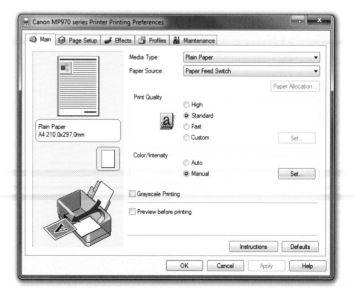

In the Main tab of the printer software, you will see the Print Quality options.

Printed Images are Dull and Lifeless

You print a picture and it doesn't look the same as it does on the monitor. It's got no sharpness or "snap" and colors are dull and indistinct.

One possibility is that you are printing at a low resolution; check this out as described on the previous page. Another, is that you are using the wrong type of paper. For example, if you want the highest quality, you need to use photo quality paper.

Furthermore, you need to tell the printer what kind of paper you are using. It may be the right type but if you don't specify it in the software, the printer will assume the currently specified paper type is loaded. Doing this is important because the printer will automatically adjust its print settings to suit the type of media being used. For example, in the case of photos it will print at the highest possible resolution.

You will find the various paper type options in the Media Type drop-down list in the software's Main tab.

Printed Colors are Wrong

Printed colors are not the same as on the monitor. This is because the monitor hasn't been set up correctly or because the printer isn't "color synchronized" with the monitor.

The first step is to calibrate the monitor so that it displays colors accurately – see pages 77-78. The second is to get the printer to use the same colors as the monitor. There are two ways to do this:

The first is to manually adjust the printer's color settings on a trial and error basis until they match those of the monitor. This is a long-winded approach that may take a lot of time, however.

The second, and easiest, is to associate the color profile that was created when you calibrated the monitor, with the printer. Do this by opening the Color Management tab in the printer software and then clicking Color Management.

This opens the Windows Color Management utility. In the "Profiles associated with this device" section, you will see the color profile that was created when you calibrated the monitor. Select it and then click "Set as Default Profile". The printer will now use the color settings associated with the monitor.

Don't forget

Before printing, you need to select the correct type of paper for the particular application. When printing photos, for example, you need to use photo-quality glossy paper.

Scanner doesn't Work

If nothing happens at all when you attempt to use the scanner, it will probably be because the system hasn't recognized it, i.e. it hasn't been installed correctly. You can check this in the Device Manager – the device should be listed in the Imaging Devices category, as shown below.

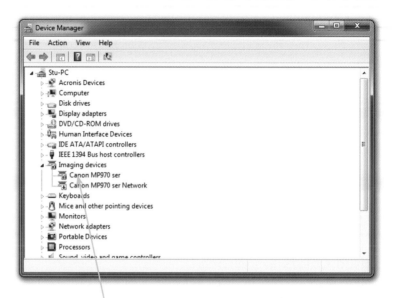

If your scanner is installed it will be listed under "Imaging devices"

Beware

With some USB scanners, subsequently relocating the interface cable to a different USB port after a successful installation can stop it from working. In this situation you need to reinstall the device's driver.

If it isn't, the first thing to check is the connections. Assuming it is a USB device (most are these days), make sure the USB cable is securely connected both to the scanner and the PC. You can also try connecting the scanner to a different USB socket.

While on the subject of USB connections, these can be the cause of another problem. This occurs when the scanner draws more power than the USB interface can deliver, and it will trigger a "USB hub power exceeded" error message.

The cause of this is having other USB powered devices connected to the system. The temporary solution is to simply disconnect as many of the other devices as is necessary to make enough power available to the scanner. For a permanent fix, you will need to buy an AC powered USB hub that will supply all the power your USB devices need.

If you are already using a USB hub and the scanner suddenly stops working, try bypassing the hub by connecting the scanner directly to the PC. If it now works, the hub is faulty.

If, after checking the connections, the scanner still isn't recognized by the system, reinstall its driver. In most cases this will resolve the problem.

If not, check the device itself. You can do this by disconnecting the interface and power cables from the scanner and then reconnecting them. The carriage on the scanner should move forward and then backward (this will be audible). Also, the internal light will come on. If neither of these things happen, you have a faulty scanner.

If the scanner appears to be OK, the next thing to check is the software being used in conjunction with it. All image editors, such as PhotoShop and PaintShop Photo Pro, provide an "Import from scanner" option and if the program being used cannot identify the correct driver for the scanner, you will get a "Scanner Initialization Failed", or similar, error message.

The solution is to manually select the correct driver from the program's Import command as shown below:

Hot tip

Something for those of you with a USB scanner to be aware of is that USB requires a driver to enable it to function. So if you get a "Scanner not found" error message when you attempt a scan, this is something else for you to check.

Open the Device Manager, and at the bottom you will see a "Universal Serial Bus controllers" category. Any problems with your USB driver will be indicated here.

Alternatively, use the scanning software supplied with the scanner. This will automatically select the correct driver.

Scanning is Slow

The first thing to say here is that if your scanner is a low-end model, you can't expect it do anything particularly well – this includes the speed at which it scans. To establish whether or not the device is simply inherently slow due to its build quality or actually has a problem, read a few online reviews – these should offer some clues.

If it does seem to be abnormally slow, the usual reason is that you are scanning your documents at too high a resolution. This means the scan heads are having to read huge amounts of data, which will of course slow the scan speed. Resolve this as follows.

In the scanner software, lower the scan resolution to 300 dpi or less. This is ample for most applications.

Scan resolution set to 300 dpi

The table below shows what scan resolutions to use for typical applications,

Application	Resolution
Images for commercial printing	300 dpi
Images to be enlarged	1200 dpi upwards
Photos for printing on inkjet printers	300 dpi
Text documents	300 dpi
Line art (drawings, diagrams, etc)	300 dpi
Images for websites	72 dpi

Scanned Files are Slow to Open

This is also caused by scanning at too high a resolution and results in a larger than necessary file size. All the file's data has to be loaded into the computer's memory before it can be viewed and, as a result, it takes a long time to open.

The solution is to rescan the document, this time at a lower resolution. The second scan will look the same as the first, but the file size will be much smaller.

To illustrate this point, a page of text scanned at 300 dpi results in a file approximately 900 KB in size while the same page scanned at 600 dpi gives a file size of some 3.5 MB – nearly four times as big. However, in terms of clarity, the two scans will be virtually indistinguishable.

Another cause can be a system low in memory. If for some reason you must scan at high resolutions, you may find that you have to upgrade your system in terms of memory capacity.

Also, remember that having other applications running at the same time as the file is being opened reduces the amount of memory available to the scanner, thus slowing things down.

Hot tip

System memory is only likely to be the cause of scanning issues in very old PCs.

Scanned Images Look Wrong

Sometimes a scanned image looks somewhat different from the original picture – it might be a lot darker, for example, or the colors may be wrong. This is usually due to a mismatch between the scanner and the monitor in terms of color, brilliance, contrast and gamma.

The solution is to either manually adjust the above settings in the scanner software on a trial and error basis until your scans look right, or associate your monitor's profile with the scanner. These procedures are the same as with the printer/monitor mismatch issue discussed on page 129.

Alternatively, you can simply adjust the images in an image editor such as PhotoShop.

This problem can also be caused by a low quality scanner and if this is the case, the only solution is to correct the images manually as mentioned above.

...cont'd

Below, we see a scanned image that is too dark being corrected in an image editor.

Image before correction   Image after correction

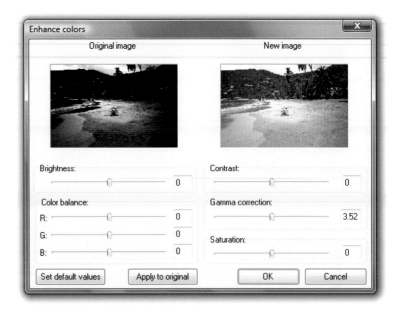

Scan Quality is Poor

Scans are blurred, blocky (pixelated), parts are missing, text and lines are broken, contain artifacts not in the original, colors are weak, etc.

These problems, and others, can be caused by a number of factors. The first is scanning at a resolution that is too low – this results in a lot of data being left out of the scan and so it looks blocky or blurred. Refer to the table on page 132 for the correct resolutions to use.

If the scanned image contains artifacts not on the original, such as spots, marks, smudges, etc; the glass scanning platen needs to be cleaned. The slightest blemish on the platen will also be scanned in, so you need to make sure it is absolutely spotless.

The document being scanned also needs to be clean. By this we mean dust, fingerprints, scratches, etc, have to be removed first.

If the document contains blemishes that cannot be removed, such as scratches and stains, see if the scanning software provides options for image enhancement, such as "Remove scratches and dust". Most do, and they can be useful for getting rid of these types of disfigurement.

Another commonly made mistake is either selecting the wrong type of document in the software, or not making a selection at all. For example, if you are scanning a color photograph, you must select "Color Photo". If you select something else, or just leave it at the default setting, the resulting scan may not look too good.

A problem that baffles many users arises when scanning documents produced on a printing press, e.g. magazines, newspapers, postcards, calendars, etc. Without going into the reasons, scans made from these types of document will contain a pattern of interference known as Moire. A typical example is shown below:

Hot tip

Moire can also be eliminated by scanning at very high resolutions. However, the trade-off will be a huge file and, for this reason, may not be a practical solution.

The solution is to select the "Magazine" or "Descreening" option in the scanning software. When this is selected, the scanner uses settings designed to get rid of, or at least reduce, Moire interference.

Text Documents Won't Edit

You've scanned a text document into your PC and now want to edit it. To do so, you copy/paste it into a word processor but find you are unable to edit the document.

The reason for this is that your "text document" is currently in an image format and, as a result, cannot be edited in a word processor. The solution is to convert the image into a text document by using an Optical Character Recognition (OCR) program.

These programs use a technique known as matrix matching that associates what the scanner perceives as being a character with a stored collection of character outlines. When a scanned character corresponds to one of these outlines, the program identifies it as the equivalent text character.

Some scanners provide an OCR program as part of the package; others however, don't, in which case a third-party program will need to be acquired. While there are many of these available for free on the Internet, the results obtained from them may not be too good. Our advice is to buy a professional package such as OmniPage Pro which, apart from providing highly accurate OCR, can also handle page elements such as borders, margins and tables.

Using OCR programs is very easy – just place the document in the scanner and click the OCR program's "Import from Scanner" button. The document will be scanned into the program and then converted automatically into a text document, which can then be pasted into your word processor.

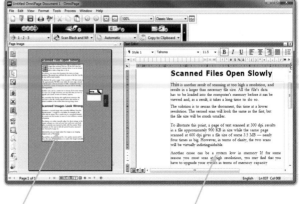

Scanned image   Image converted to a text document

Digital Camera Issues

One of the big advantages of digital photography is that it enables users to edit their photos on a PC. However, this can only be done if you can get the pictures into the computer in the first place. This potential problem is what we'll look at first.

Pictures Won't Download to the PC

When you connect the camera to the PC, Windows AutoPlay feature should open automatically. From here, you can access the camera's memory card. Alternatively, if you go to Start, My Computer, your camera should be listed here.

If neither of these happen, the PC is not "seeing" your camera. Check this out as follows:

- Check the camera is switched on – if it isn't, the PC won't see it. (Don't forget that most digicams have a power saving mode that switches the device off after a few minutes of inactivity.)

- Some cameras must be set to the image viewing mode in order to be detected by the computer. Check that you have done this

- Check that the USB transfer cable is connected to both the camera and the PC

- Connect the USB cable to a different USB socket on the PC (it is possible for a USB socket to be faulty)

- If the USB cable is connected to a USB hub, bypass the hub by connecting it directly to the PC

- Your camera may require a driver to be installed in order for the computer to detect the camera. Install the driver according the manufacturer's instructions (also, check the manufacturer's website for an updated driver)

If you still can't get a connection to the PC, there is a fault with either the camera, the camera's memory card or the USB cable.

The first one to check is the USB cable. Do this by trying a different one. Then replace the memory card. If you still can't get a connection, the camera has to be faulty.

Don't forget

Before a digital camera will download pictures to a computer it must be switched on. Don't overlook this obvious step. Also, some cameras need to be set to a specific mode before they can communicate with Windows. Check your camera documentation to confirm this if you are unsure.

Hot tip

Windows operating systems provide native USB support. However, it may not be compatible with your digicam's software. If this is the case, you may need to download an update to the software from the manufacturer's website.

...cont'd

Problems with Your Pictures

Having got your pictures onto your PC, you may find that they don't look quite as good as you expected. This can be for any number of reasons and the following are the ones most commonly experienced:

Images are Blurred

There are three causes of blurred pictures:

- Camera motion

- Subject motion

- Incorrect focus

This problem is most pronounced with cheaper digicams, which tend to have slow shutter speeds. To avoid camera motion, you must hold the camera as steady as possible while taking the shot. The best way to do this is to use the viewfinder (assuming there is one) to compose the shot (it is harder to hold the camera steady when you have it out at arm's length and are using the LCD).

If there is motion in the scene being snapped, you must either use the appropriate preset setting – see your camera documentation – or manually select a faster shutter speed (assuming this option is available).

The other possibility is that the subject is out of focus. The best way around this problem is to let your camera "prefocus" on your subject by holding the shutter control halfway down for a moment before taking the shot.

Pixelated or Grainy Images

If your pictures have a blocky, pixelated appearance, the reason will be that the camera is set to a low-resolution mode. Locate the setting that allows you to change the resolution and set it to a higher level.

However, when doing this you should be aware that the higher the resolution you select, the larger the size of each picture file. This in turn means that the camera's memory card will have room for fewer pictures.

For general use, mid-range resolution (usually denoted as "Standard" in the camera's settings, will be quite adequate.

Noise

Another common problem is noise, which gives pictures a grainy look. This is most likely to be experienced when the camera is used in poorly lit conditions, and with high zoom settings.

In the former scenario, the camera will automatically select a high ISO setting (this is the measurement of the camera's sensitivity to light) to compensate for the lack of light. Without going into the reasons, the drawback is that the higher the ISO setting, the more noise introduced into the image. The solution is to set the camera's ISO setting to manual and then experiment with lower settings.

Hot tip

Dark scenes, such as those taken at night, are more likely to be grainy, as the camera will have to use a higher ISO setting.

Using a digital camera's zoom function may also be the cause of noisy pictures. Most cameras offer both digital and optical zoom, with digital offering a greater distance range. Unfortunately, due to the techniques used in digital zooming, noise is an unavoidable side effect. Although you won't be able to zoom as far with the optical mode, unwanted noise will be much less of a problem.

Images Are Under- or Over-Exposed

If *all* your images suffer from this problem, the cause is probably not the camera, but simply that the brightness control on your monitor is incorrectly adjusted.

If under-exposure is peculiar to your indoor shots, or outside shots taken at night, then either you haven't used the camera's flash or the scene was beyond the effective range of the flash. Note that digicams typically have a maximum flash range of about nine feet.

If just parts of outdoor or complex scenes are too dark or light (not the entire picture, note), the usual cause is that the prevailing lighting conditions have misled the camera's light meter into under- or over-exposing the shot.

One solution to this is to use the camera's flash fill mode to illuminate the dark sections of a scene. However, as we mentioned above, flash guns have a limited range so it will have to be a close-up shot for this to be effective.

A better way to is simply to adjust the direction from which you take the shot so that the light source is behind you rather than the subject. Remember, when the light source is behind your subject it will appear too dark, almost like a silhouette.

...cont'd

Poor Color

Color is a difficult element of a picture to get right with digital cameras and there are several reasons for this.

The most likely one is that your camera's white balance is incorrect. White balance is a means of calibrating a camera to record true white correctly. As all other colors produced by the camera are based on the white balance, if it is incorrect all other colors will also be incorrect.

Digital cameras are set to automatic white balance by default and this does a very good job under most circumstances. However, there are times when the white balance needs to be changed manually to match the prevailing lighting conditions in order to obtain more true-to-life colors in a photo.

To this end, most digital cameras provide a range of white balance presets – typically Tungsten, Daylight, Cloudy, Flash and Shade. These enable the user to instruct the camera how to handle the lighting conditions.

However, while results are reasonable, they are never optimal. If you are serious about your digital photography, to get the best out of your pictures in terms of color, you need to set the white balance manually. It is beyond the scope of this book to explain how to do this but you will find many websites and books such as *Digital Photography in easy steps* that provide full instructions.

Imaging Software

While most image quality issues can be corrected at source with the camera's settings, the many users for whom camera terminology is double dutch may find that it is easier to do it manually with the aid of an image editor such as Photoshop or Adobe Lightroom.

In fact, with cheaper cameras, the use of these programs can be the only way to correct some image defects. While top-end programs such as Photoshop are very expensive, there are many less expensive alternatives that provide the necessary options.

Hot tip

As a general rule, presets, while producing decent results, are never as good as a manually set up camera.

Hot tip

A very good (and much cheaper) alternative to Photoshop is Adobe Photoshop Elements.

The Mouse doesn't Work

The cause of this problem depends on what type of mouse you are using.

If it is the old-fashioned mechanical ball and wheel type, you almost certainly have a bad connection to the PC – there's little else to go wrong.

Check that the cable is connected to the green PS/2 mouse port at the rear of the computer. Note that the purple port below, or to the side, and which is otherwise identical, is for the keyboard. It is very easy to connect the mouse to this port by mistake.

Hot tip

If the mouse uses the PS/2 port, you must switch the PC off before unplugging it or plugging it in. USB mice, however, can be connected with the PC running.

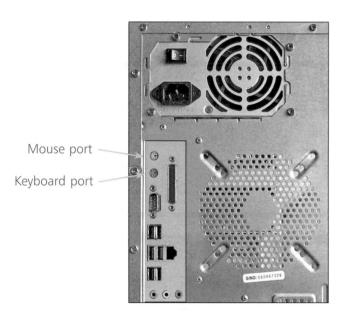

Mouse port

Keyboard port

If the mouse is a USB model, try connecting it to a different USB socket. If it is connected via a USB hub, bypass the hub by connecting the mouse directly to a USB port.

Hot tip

Cordless mice have a limited range – typically about nine feet.

If you are using a wireless (cordless) mouse, another possibility is that the radio frequency connection between the mouse and its receiver has been lost. Resolve this by removing the batteries from the mouse and then replacing them.

Doing this will automatically reinstate the radio connection (note that you may also have to press a button on the mouse or the receiver – see the mouse documentation).

Mouse Operation is Poor

Poor mouse operation can mean slow, intermittent or erratic movement of the pointer.

With a mechanical ball and wheel mouse, the problem will be due to a build-up of dirt on the internal wheels. Open the device and simply scrape the dirt away. The mouse will then be as good as new.

If you are using an optical or laser mouse, use a cotton swab or cleaning bud to clean the plastic LED covering. Any dirt here may inhibit correct operation of the LED and the associated sensor.

LED on the underside of the mouse

In the case of a cordless mouse, check for external devices that may be interfering with the radio signal. Items such as wireless routers, radios, cell phones, desktop fans, fluorescent lights, and large metal objects like computer cases and metal furniture may interfere with the signal.

If any of the above are within 12 inches of the mouse, move them further away.

Poor mouse operation can also be caused by batteries that are on the point of dying.

11 Security

Security on a PC takes various forms. Here, we take a brief look at how to deal with viruses, and an in-depth look at how to keep your data safe, and conceal your browsing tracks.

Dealing with a Virus

Virus Symptoms

Of all the various security issues that PC users can face, viruses and malware can be the most difficult to resolve. Very often, users aren't even aware that their system is infected. So we'll start with a list of typical symptoms of viral infection:

- The PC becomes unstable, e.g. crashes, locks-up, and reboots without warning

- The PC runs slower than usual

- Error and warning messages appear

- Toolbars appear in your web browser

- The CD/DVD drive tray opens and closes by itself

- The websites of anti-virus companies are inaccessible

- Your web browser automatically redirects to advertising sites

If you find yourself with any of the above issues, the first thing you should do is to terminate your Internet connection, particularly if you have passwords and log-on details stored on the PC. Then run an up-to-date anti-virus program; if you don't have any, go out and buy one.

This should resolve the issue. However, you may find that it does not, in which case the problem is likely to be caused by malware. The solution is the same as for viruses – buy an anti-malware program. Note that while modern anti-virus software claims to offer protection against malware as well as viruses, in practice a dedicated anti-malware program will usually offer better protection.

Sources of Viruses

Having got rid of the virus, you may be interested to know how it got there in the first place so as to prevent a repeat of the issue. There are, in fact, many ways in which viruses can be placed on a computer and the most common of these are:

- Downloading freeware and shareware programs from the Internet. Many of these applications will be loaded with a virus that runs when the program's setup file is opened

- Downloading software, music and video files from file sharing (peer-to-peer) networks

- Opening attachments to email messages

- Running serial number generators (known as keygens) for illegally acquired software

Avoiding Virus Infection

The easiest way of preventing any of the above actions from infecting your PC is to simply not do them. If you must though, scan the file with an anti-virus and an anti-malware program.

Another problem you may experience when browsing the web is a dialog box popping up in your browser that contains a message of some kind. For example, it may inform you that it is an anti-virus program and that it has detected a virus on your PC. If you click a button, it will remove it for you. Whatever you do, do not click the button – it will download a virus on to your PC.

If you try to close the dialog box, either it will refuse to close or just keep re-opening as fast as you close it. Also, all the browser controls may be disabled so you have no way of closing it. To get out of this situation press Ctrl+Alt+Delete, which will open the Task Manager. In the Applications tab, right-click your browser and click End Task.

Problems of this type are often the result of browsing sites you shouldn't be browsing. For example, illegal software download sites and sites offering software hacks and cracks.

Another issue that can afflict unprotected PCs is hacking. This comes about when the user doesn't have a firewall in place which, without going into the details, means the PC's software ports are open and, thus, so is the PC. Anyone with the requisite knowledge can exploit these open ports to place software on a PC, browse it as though it was their own PC, and even take it over completely.

The user is never aware that any of this is going on. To prevent this happening, all that is required is a firewall application that monitors the PC's ports for any signs of intrusion and blocks any that it finds.

Keep Your Data Safe

Many computer users keep sensitive data on their PC that they don't want anyone else to have access to. Assuming this applies to you, how do you go about it? Well, there are actually several methods with which you can secure your data, and the easiest is to simply restrict access to Windows. This can be done in three ways:

Set a Boot Password

All BIOS setup programs provide an option to password-protect the bootup procedure. To do this, start the PC and enter the BIOS setup program as described on page 33.

On the opening screen you should see an option to "Set User Password". Select this and enter a password; this password-protects the BIOS setup program. Then look for a security option (usually found in the Advanced BIOS Features page). This enables you to set a boot password. Do so, save the changes and exit the BIOS. When you restart the PC, you will be asked to enter the password; without it the boot procedure will stop at this point.

Set an Account Logon Password

This method requires a password to be entered before the desktop can be accessed. The option to set a password is offered during Window's installation procedure. If you didn't do it then, do it now as described below:

1 Click Start, Control Panel, User Accounts

Hot tip

In case you forget your logon password, you can make a password reset disk. This is explained on page 149.

2 Click "Create a password for your account"

3 Enter and confirm your password

Use an Encrypted Password Disk

This is an extremely secure method of restricting access to a PC by using an encrypted key.

<u>WARNING</u>: The procedure cannot be undone. Be quite sure that you need this level of security before you start.

1 Type syskey in the Start menu search box and press Enter

2 In the dialog box that opens, click Update

3 Tick "System Generated Password" and then "Store Startup Key on Floppy Disk"

4 Insert a floppy disk when prompted. An encrypted key will be saved to the disk

From this point on, every time you boot the PC, it will be necessary to insert the disk into the floppy drive before you can access the logon screen. So just make sure you don't lose it, otherwise you won't be able to access your own computer.

Beware

If you lose the disk containing the encrypted key, you will be locked out of your own PC. So make a backup copy of the disk and store it in a separate location.

147

Hot tip

If your system doesn't have a floppy drive, you can use a USB flash drive instead. However, you will first need to assign the A drive letter to the USB drive. Instructions on how to do this can be found on the Internet.

...cont'd

Password-Protect Your Folders

With access to the operating system secured, the really security-conscious user may want to make things even more difficult for a potential intruder. The way to do this is to password-protect any sensitive data so that even if someone does manage to gain entry to the PC, they can't get to your data. Unfortunately, Windows 7 doesn't provide a folder password-protection function.

The only option therefore, is to use a third-party application. Do a Google search and you will find dozens of programs of this type. A typical example is one called Folder Password Protect, which is available from www.protect-folders.com. This simple but effective application lets you password-protect any number of folders, either individually or collectively, by adding them to a main window, as shown below:

Click Next, and in the new dialog box enter the desired password. Click OK and you're done - the selected folder, or folders, are protected. To unlock a folder, click it and enter the password. It couldn't be simpler

Beware

A badly written password-protection utility can be more dangerous (in terms of data protection) than not having one at all. If it is buggy, you could well end up losing your data. For this reason, give freeware and shareware programs a definite miss.

148

Safeguard Your Passwords

Having password-protected your system and data, if you now go and lose or forget a password, you'll wish you'd never bothered with it in the first place. This is very easy to do, particularly if you have several. So you need to guard against this possibility.

We'll start with your account password; Windows makes this a snap. All you will need is a removable disk or drive – this can be a floppy disk, CD/DVD or a flash drive.

1 Click User Accounts in the Control Panel and on the left, click "Create a password reset disk"

2 The Forgotten Password wizard launches – simply follow the prompts until the procedure is done. An encrypted key will be written to your disk/flash drive

Should you subsequently lose the password, you can use the disk to set a new password that will replace the original one.

While that takes care of the logon password, you will undoubtedly have several others, including your Internet passwords, e.g. eBay. Unfortunately, Windows does not provide a utility that can be used to safely store and manage passwords.

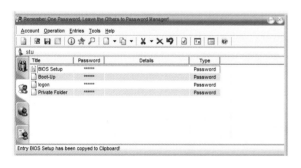

So what we suggest is that you acquire a Password Manager program.

The easiest way is to download one from the Internet; you will find dozens – some free, some not. The one shown above, Password Manager, is a typical example.

These programs work by hiding the passwords behind asterisks; a mouse click is required to reveal them. Thus, malicious software will not be able to see what they are. Password managers are themselves password-protected to prevent physical access by a snooper. So all you have to do is remember a single password.

Beware

Keep your password-reset disk in a safe place. If someone else gets hold of it, they will be able to access your account by setting a new password that will overwrite the previous one. They'll be in and you'll be out.

Hot tip

Good password managers have an auto-fill facility, similar to Internet Explorer's AutoComplete. It should also be possible to install and run them from removable media. A good example is RoboForm, which can be run from a flash drive.

...cont'd

Data Encryption

We've seen how to secure your data by password-protecting both it and the PC. What we haven't considered yet is the possibility of someone cracking your password. The answer to this is to encrypt the data itself, thus adding a further layer of protection.

Windows 7 provides data encryption via its Encrypting File System (EFS) feature and it's very easy to use. Simply right-click the folder containing data to be encrypted, click Properties and then the Advanced button. In the dialog box that opens, select "Encrypt contents to secure data". The names of the files in the folder will then change to green to signify that they are encrypted.

However, even though it is encrypted, the data is still vulnerable to someone who either physically steals the entire PC, or the drive the data is stored on. This is due to the fact that EFS only works on drives formatted with the NTFS file system, so if the encrypted folder is copied to a non-NTFS drive, the encryption is removed and the data will thus be accessible.

To guard against this, you need to use another feature provided by Windows 7. This is called BitLocker Drive Encryption and it provides "offline" data protection by making it possible to encrypt an entire drive (including removable USB flash drives).

Go to Start, Control Panel and click BitLocker Drive Encryption. Click "Turn On BitLocker" next to the drive to be encrypted and then follow the prompts – this will include setting a password to unlock the drive. Note that the encryption process can take a very long time. When it is finished, if you go to My Computer, you will see that the encrypted drive now has a padlocked drive icon.

Hot tip

Note that BitLocker cannot be used on a single file or folder. You have to encrypt the entire drive that contains the data to be protected.

If you remove the drive and then re-install it, a dialog box will pop-up asking for the password, as shown on the left. To remove encryption or set a different method of unlocking the drive, re-open the utility and select "Manage BitLocker".

Backup Your Data

The final way in which your data can be compromised is losing it. This can be accidental deletion, a virus attack, hardware or operating system failure, or data corruption.

As a safeguard against any of these potential threats, you need to create a backup on a separate medium. Apart from the medium itself, this requires a backup program. With Windows 7, Microsoft have provided a Backup utility that is not only extremely simple to use but is also very effective.

Access it by going to Start, Control Panel, Backup and Restore. In the main window, you will see a "Backup now" button. Click this and by default, the utility backs up all data files, such as documents, images, videos, etc.

When enabled, it runs automatically at a time and frequency specified by the user and simply updates the previous backup. You can also specify types of file not to be included. The backup can be used to restore everything or just selected files.

Hot tip

You can only make backups to a separate drive or partition. If you don't have a second drive, or one of sufficient capacity, we suggest you create a second partition on your existing hard drive and use this as the backup location.

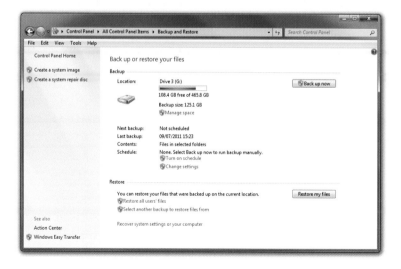

At the top-left you also will see an option to create a system image. This will build a mirror image of whichever drive, or drives, you select.

Should you have a catastrophic failure of Windows or a hard drive failure, this can be used to restore your computer to exactly how it was when the backup was made.

...cont'd

It is entirely up to you whether or not you do this, but as it only takes a few minutes and provides you with a guaranteed method of restoring your system, we highly recommend that you do.

1 Click "Create a system image". This opens the dialog box shown below. The utility will now look for a suitable backup medium – see margin note. Then click Next

2 A new dialog box will open asking you to specify which drive, or drives, you want to image. Make your selection and click Next

3 Confirm your settings and click Start backup

Keep Your Activities Private

Security on a PC is not just about keeping your data safe; it can also be about keeping your computing activities private. While there are many reasons for doing this, it's not so easy to actually do as Windows keeps records of user activity in several places. Anyone who knows where to look can find out what websites you've visited, files you've accessed, programs you've been using, etc. If you're not careful, they can even access your password-protected web pages.

The following are the most common give-aways:

Jump Lists

When you right-click a program's icon on the Taskbar, a jump list of files recently opened with that program will be revealed, as shown right.

If you have been using Microsoft Word to type a letter to your Bank Manager, for example, a subsequent user will be able to see the name of the file in the jump list and also open it. You can prevent this as follows:

1. Right-click the Taskbar and click Properties. Then click the Start Menu tab

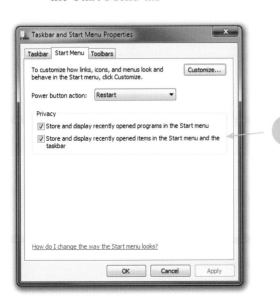

2. Uncheck "Store and display recently opened items in the Start menu and the taskbar"

Hot tip

Items in jump lists can be deleted individually by right-clicking and then clicking "Remove from this list". However, one day you will forget to do it. This tip provides a permanent solution so you don't have to keep checking that you've done it.

153

Frequently Used Programs List

A feature introduced with XP and continued with Windows 7 is the Frequently Used Programs list. This list updates automatically according to the frequency with which programs are run.

There are several ways of dealing with this. The first is to simply right-click an entry and click "Remove from this list". However, it may not be long before it is back again, so this is not an ideal solution.

A more effective way is to disable the feature permanently so you can just forget about it.

Hot tip

Another way is to click the Customize button on the Start Menu tab of the "Taskbar and Start Menu Properties" dialog box. Here, you will be able to specify the number of recent programs to display. If you select 0, none will be displayed.

154

1   Right-click the Start button and click Properties. Then click the Start Menu tab

2   Uncheck "Store and display recently opened programs in the Start menu"

However, doing this will leave the Start Menu with a large blank area that you may not like the look of. Alternatively, you may find the feature useful and would rather just prevent certain applications appearing on the list. In either case, do the following:

1 Open the Registry Editor and locate the following key: HKEY_CLASSES_ROOT\Applications\Program name. exe ("Program name.exe" is the program you want to block, e.g. PhotoShop as shown below)

2 Click the program's folder and in the right-hand window, right-click and select New, String Value. Name it NoStartPage

3 If the program you want isn't listed under Applications, right-click the Applications folder and select New, Key. Give the key the same name as the program's executable file (see margin note). Then follow the procedure described in Step 2

Reboot the PC. The application in question will now never be displayed on the Frequently Used Programs list – very handy for hiding from the boss the fact that you play Freecell all day.

Hot tip

To find the name of a program's executable file (the file you click to open it), click the hard drive in My Computer and then open the Program Files folder.

Locate the program you want, open its folder and look in the Type column; the type you are looking for is "Application". Alongside this in the Name column will be the program's executable file name.

When you name the key (Step 3) don't forget to add .exe after the program's name. For example: PhotoShop.exe.

155

Most Recently Used Lists (MRUs)

The most common method of preventing other users from seeing a private file is to simply squirrel it away in a location that is not likely to be accessed by someone else – out of sight, out of mind, as the saying goes.

However, while a file hidden in this way may be difficult to physically locate, there is a way for another user to easily find it.

This is courtesy of the Most Recently Used files feature, found in most programs, that enables a user to reopen a recent file quickly without having to go to its location.

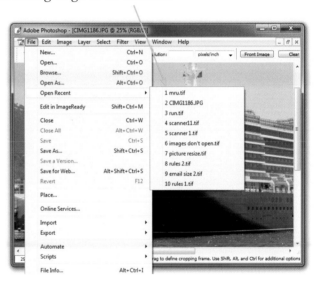

So a user looking to keep a particular file private will need to clear the MRU list in any program it has been accessed with recently – see margin note.

Windows Searches

Another method of finding data is using the Windows Search utility. No matter how well a user hides a file, if another user specifies that file type in a search, the file will be revealed.

For example, if someone was to type .doc into a folder's search box, all Microsoft Word documents in the folder, including sub-folders, would be revealed. The problem here is that there is no way to configure the Search utility to prevent another user from searching for a file of a specific type.

The only way, in fact, to prevent files being revealed by Windows Searches is to place them in a password-protected folder.

Users running Windows XP are able to password-protect folders but this functionality has been removed in Windows 7. The only way to do it therefore, is to install a third-party utility (see page 148).

Run Command History

The Run command is hidden by default in Windows 7. However, if you, or another user, has added it to the Start Menu (see margin note), be aware that it keeps a history. This can reveal to other users what programs, folders, documents, and even web pages, you have accessed.

Hot tip

You can restore the Run command to the Start Menu by right-clicking the Taskbar and clicking Properties. Then click the Start Menu tab and click Customize. Scroll down to Run Command and check the box.

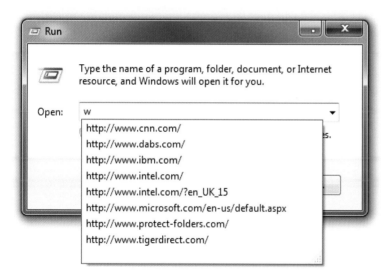

For example, someone typing the letter W into the Run box will see a list of all the web pages that have been accessed since the history folder was last cleared. Furthermore, by selecting a page and clicking OK, the web page will be opened in the PC's browser.

There is a registry setting that will clear the Run history, but an easier way is to download and install a program called MRU-Blaster from www.javacoolsoftware.com. This is a free utility that will clear not only the Windows Run History but also program MRUs (see page 156).

Hot tip

The Run command's history is automatically cleared every time the PC is shut down.

Hide Your Browsing Tracks

Browsing History

In the same way that Windows keeps records of user activity, so does Internet Explorer.

This information is held in the following places:

- History Folder – this folder holds a chronological record of every website and page visited

- Temporary Internet Files Folder – this folder is a cache of the pages you have accessed. Should you revisit a particular web page, your browser will retrieve it from this cache rather than from the Web. This makes access to the page quicker

- Cookies Folder – cookies are text files that websites download to your PC. They have several purposes; one is to identify you should you visit that website again. Often, they will also reveal the type of website, e.g. stuart@luckydollarcasino

For users who wish to keep their Internet activities private, Internet Explorer provides a Delete Browsing History option. To access it, open Internet Explorer, click the Tools button and then "Delete Browsing History".

Alternatively, you can configure Internet Explorer to delete its browsing history by default. Go to Start, Control Panel, Internet Options. On the General tab, check "Delete browsing history on exit".

Beware

Don't forget to check your Internet Favorites. When accessed, certain websites will place a link to their website here. Common culprits in this respect are porn websites. Anyone who happens to use your browser may see anything which has been added in this way.

158

Don't forget

The three folders that can give the game away for you are: the Temporary Internet Files folder, the History folder and the Cookies folder.

AutoComplete

Internet Explorer has a feature called AutoComplete that enables the browser to automatically enter web addresses, user-names, passwords, and data entered on web-based forms. This can be convenient as it saves the user from having to type out this information each time.

However, it can also be dangerous as it allows other people to access your password-protected pages, and see what data you've entered in forms, etc. It will also enable any snooper to see which websites you have visited, and any keywords entered in search engine search boxes.

If you wish to keep this type of information private then you need to disable AutoComplete or alter its settings.

1 Go to Start, Control Panel, Internet Options. Click the Contents tab

2 Click Settings in the AutoComplete section

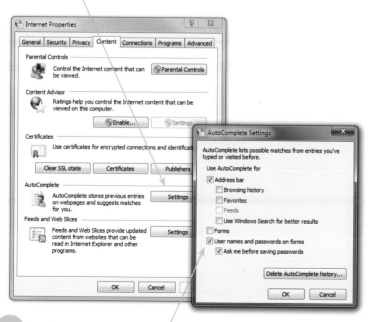

3 Remove the checks from "Address Bar" and "User names and passwords on forms"

...cont'd

InPrivate Browsing

As we have seen on the previous page, it is possible to delete your browsing history after the session. However, there are two problems with this approach:

1) You may forget to do it

2) You have to delete the entire history when maybe all you want to do is to delete a small part of it – it's an all-or-nothing action

The solution is a new feature in Internet Explorer 8 called InPrivate browsing. When used, InPrivate temporarily suspends Internet Explorer's automatic caching functions and, at the same time, keeps your previous browsing history intact. A typical example of when you might want to do this is buying a gift online for a loved one; once done, you can revert to browsing as normal. Your browsing history up to the point of opening the InPrivate session is kept but the InPrivate session itself is not.

There are two ways of using this feature:

1 In Internet Explorer, click Tools on the menu bar and select InPrivate Browsing. A new browser window will open. Use this for your InPrivate session

If you don't see the menu bar in your browser, right-click on the blue section at the top of the window and click Menu Bar.

Beware

While InPrivate Browsing keeps other people who use your computer from seeing what sites you've visited, it does not prevent someone on your network, such as a network administrator.

Beware

InPrivate Browsing does not provide you with anonymity on the Internet. For example, websites might be able to identify you through your web address. Also anything you do on a website can be recorded by that website.

2 Right-click Internet Explorer on the Taskbar and select InPrivate. This will open an InPrivate session

A handy tip for those who will do a lot of InPrivate browsing is to configure Internet Explorer to open InPrivate by default. Do this as follows:

1 Right-click the Desktop and select New, Shortcut

2 In the "Location of the Item" box, type: **"C:\Program Files (x86)\Internet Explorer\iexplore.exe" -private**. Click Next, give the shortcut a name and save it in a convenient location

Hot tip

Note that there is a space between .exe" and -private.

Hide Your Drives

The following procedure does more than just hide a file or folder: it actually hides the drive the file/folder is located on.

1 Start the Registry Editor and locate the following key: HKEY_CURRENT_USER\Software\Microsoft\ Windows\CurrentVersion\Policies

2 Right-click the Policies folder and click New, Key. Name the new key Explorer

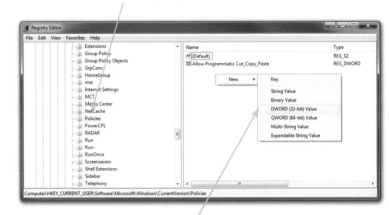

3 Click the Explorer folder and on the right, right-click and select New, DWORD. Name it NoDrives. Right-click NoDrives and in the Value Data box, enter the number of the drive (shown in the table below) to be hidden. Then exit the registry editor and reboot the PC

Drive A – 1	Drive J – 512	Drive S – 262144
Drive B – 2	Drive K – 1024	Drive T – 524288
Drive C – 4	Drive L – 2048	Drive U – 1048576
Drive D – 8	Drive M – 4096	Drive V – 2097152
Drive E – 16	Drive N – 8192	Drive W – 4194304
Drive F – 32	Drive O – 16384	Drive X – 8388608
Drive G – 64	Drive P – 32768	Drive Y – 16777216
Drive H – 128	Drive Q – 65536	Drive Z – 33554432
Drive I – 256	Drive R – 131072	All – 67108863

12 Files and Folders

In this chapter, we troubleshoot a range of common problems experienced when working with files and Windows folders.

You are Unable to Delete a File

You right-click a file and click Delete but it refuses to go. There are several possible causes for this behavior but the most common one is that the file is in use. In this situation you will get an error message as shown below.

If the error message specifies the program that the file is open in as in the example above, fairly obviously the first thing is to close this program. If it doesn't specify the program, close all programs that you can see are open – these will be indicated on the Taskbar. Then try deleting the file again.

If it still won't go, reboot the computer. This will forcibly close all running programs on the computer. On restart, you should be able to delete the file.

However, there are rare situations in which even this won't work. In so, reboot the computer into Safe Mode as described on page 37. In the vast majority of cases, you will then be able to delete the file. Then reboot back into the normal Windows mode.

In the unlikely event that the file still refuses to go, it has almost certainly been created by a virus. Run your anti-virus program to get rid of it.

Hot tip

When faced with a really stubborn file, deleting when in Safe Mode is usually the answer.

A File Opens in the Wrong Program

As an example, you click an image file but instead of opening in the usual imaging program, it opens in a different one.

The reason for this is that another program has configured itself as the default application for opening files of that type. Many programs do this when they are installed.

However, you can easily reinstate your favored program as the default as described below:

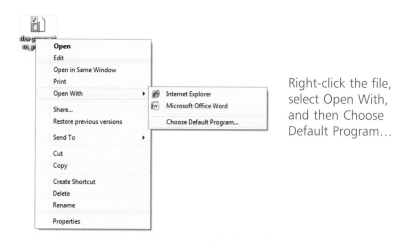

Right-click the file, select Open With, and then Choose Default Program…

Hot tip

Most programs will let the user choose whether or not to make them the default program. The option will be offered during the installation procedure.

If your desired program is listed, select it and click OK. Otherwise click Browse…

...cont'd

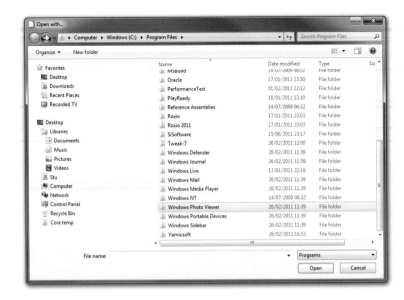

Go to the Program Files folder, locate the folder of the program you want as the default and open it

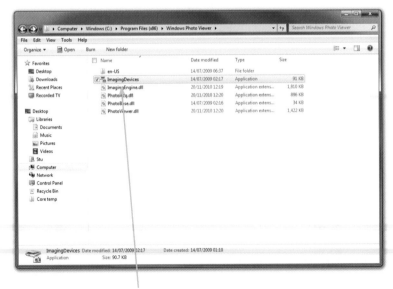

Don't forget

When setting a program as the default, you must select its executable file.

Select the program's executable file. This will be denoted by the word "Application" in the Type column.

Your file will now always open with the selected program.

A File won't Open

You click a file but it doesn't open. You might get an error message that may or may not provide a clue as to the cause of the problem. Alternatively, nothing happens at all.

The most likely reasons are:

The File is Corrupt (Damaged)

In this situation, unless the file is included in a backup you have previously made, there is nothing you can do to restore it to a working condition. If it has been backed up, though, you will be able to restore it (if you don't know how, just follow the instructions in the backup program's Help file).

Users of Windows 7 and Vista have another option. This is the Previous Versions utility – see pages 172–173.

A Compatible Program Isn't Installed on the PC

If a program capable of opening the file isn't installed on the PC, you will get the error message shown below:

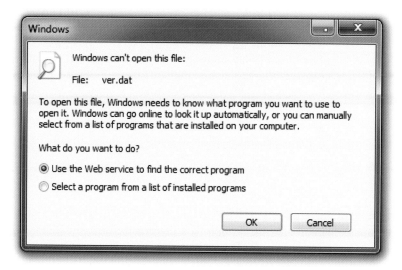

If you know which program is required, you will have to install it in order to open the file. If you don't know, select the first option, "Use the Web service to find the appropriate program". This takes you to a Microsoft website from where you may be able to identify programs compatible with the file.

However, there are many sites that offer a more comprehensive list of file extensions. For example, try www.sharpened.net/extensions.

...cont'd

This site has a large database of known file types and the programs that can open them. Simply select the file type of the file that won't open and you will be presented with a list of programs with which the file is compatible.

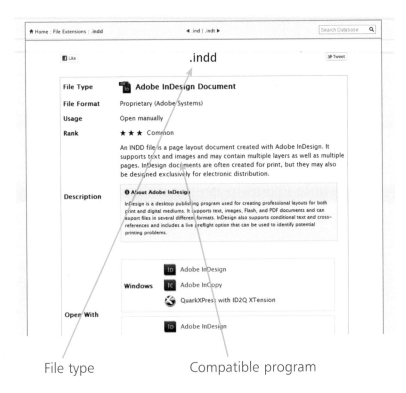

File type   Compatible program

Now all you have to do is acquire the program in order to open your file.

The File is Incompatible with the Program Version

When they create a new version of a program, most software manufacturers ensure that it is compatible with previous versions, i.e. that files created with the earlier versions will open with the new version and vice versa.

However, at some stage in the evolution of a program, due to technical advances, it becomes necessary to abandon support for some of the earliest versions. Incompatibility is the result. In this situation your only option is to find an older version of the program. There are quite a few websites that offer older versions of commonly used software, e.g. www.oldapps.com.

You are Unable to Locate a File

To enable users to find data on their PCs, all versions of Windows provide a search utility. We'll look at the one provided by Windows 7.

This, not surprisingly, is called Search and it is a considerable improvement on the versions supplied with previous incarnations of Windows. One of the reasons for this is that the utility is tightly integrated in the operating system, as a result of which it is instantly accessible from virtually any location. You will find it on the Start Menu and in any Explorer folder.

One of its best features is that it is contextual, i.e. its search is based on the user's current activity, whether it's searching for utilities in the Control Panel, for music files in Windows Media Player or for files and applications in the Start menu.

When doing a search with Windows 7, you have three ways to go:

First, do a folder search; this is the best option if you already know which folder the file is located in. Simply enter the name of the file in the search box at the top-right of the relevant folder window and the utility will search the folder and display the results of the search. (Note that, by default, the search will be restricted to the contents of the folder, including sub-folders.)

Hot tip

A folder search will only find content that is located in the folder the search is conducted from. Don't use this for a system-wide search.

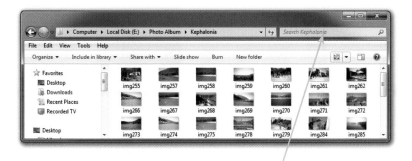

Folder search box

Second, use the Search utility on the Start Menu as shown on the next page. This option will search the entire computer.

...cont'd

Don't forget

To search the entire computer, use the Start Menu Search utility.

If you have limited identifying information about a file, left-click in the search box and you will see 4 search filters. These enable you to search by Kind, Date modified, Type and Size. For example, if you specify .doc, (the file extension for Microsoft Word documents) with the Type filter, your search will return all Word documents on the PC.

While using these filters is unlikely to pinpoint an individual file, they will produce a narrowed-down list. This should be small enough to search through relatively quickly.

The third way is to use the Start Menu search box. With this option you can locate not only files and folders, but also programs, emails and offline web pages.

Explorer Folders Are Missing

In previous versions of Windows, system folders such as the Recycle Bin and the Control Panel are displayed on the left-hand side of Explorer windows. This makes them quickly accessible.

In Windows 7, these folders are not displayed. Getting them back is quite easy, however.

Open any Explorer folder and click Tools on the menu bar. Then click Folder Options.

Check "Show all folders". Click OK and your top-level system folders will now be visible in all Windows.

You can also add any other folder you may want to be accessible in this way. Open an Explorer window and then click Favorites on the left-hand side. In the window that opens, simply drag-and-drop the required folder. It will now appear in the Favorites list.

Hot tip

You can also remove a folder by right-clicking on it and clicking Remove.

Above, we have created a link to the author's photo album.

Recovering a Deleted File

You've deleted a file, either by accident or design, and now wish to get it back.

Your first option is to check the Recycle Bin (located on the desktop) – this is a folder that Windows uses as a cache for all deleted data. All files that you delete will be placed here – they're not actually deleted at all. This gives you a chance to get the file back should you change your mind.

Simply open the Recycle Bin, right-click the file and click Restore – it will be restored to its original location.

Third-Party Utilities

However, if you have already emptied the Recycle Bin things become much more tricky. It may still be possible to restore the file but this will require the use of a third-party utility.

To understand this, you need to be aware that when a file is deleted its contents will still be on the hard drive until the space it is occupying is overwritten by data subsequently written to the drive. For example, if you delete a file and then immediately create a new one, there is a good chance that the new file will overwrite the deleted one. When this happens, it will be gone for good.

So the first rule when in this situation is not to create any more files or install programs (if you do, you may overwrite the file you wish to recover). You will have to buy a file recovery program that is capable of recovering data from the hard drive.

Run the recovery program from the installation disk (don't install it, for the reason already mentioned) and it should be able to recover your file.

Previous Versions Utility

Users of Windows 7 and Vista have another option available to them – the Previous Versions utility. Not only can this recover deleted files, it can also restore modified and damaged files to their original state.

The application is integrated with the Backup, and System Restore, utilities and it uses the data saved in backups and system restore points. For the feature to work, i.e. for previous versions of a file to be available, you must have at least one of these utilities enabled.

Hot tip

Data recovery programs either allow you to run the program from the installation disk or create a recovery disc (floppy, CD or flash drive).
   In either case, this allows you to use the program without having to install it on the hard drive (which would overwrite the file you wish to recover).

Beware

While there are many file recovery programs available for download on the Internet, these have to be installed on the PC. The action of doing so may overwrite the file you want to recover. Therefore, you need to buy one that can be run from the installation disk.

In operation it's quite straightforward. In the case of a damaged or modified file that you want to restore, simply right-click the file and click Restore Previous Versions.

You'll see a list of available previous versions of the file. These will either be shadow copies (taken from a system restore point), backup copies (taken from a backup), or both.

Beware

If you restore a file, it will replace the current version. As this cannot be undone, make sure there is nothing in the current version that you want to keep. If there is, copy it elsewhere first.

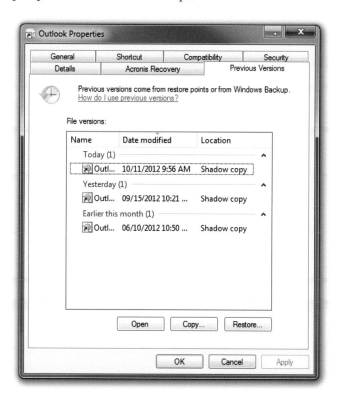

To restore a file, select it and then click the Restore button. If it's a backup copy, a Restore Files wizard will open – just follow the prompts.

If it's a shadow copy, the file will be restored immediately – this is the quicker of the two options.

In the case of a deleted file that you want to recover, right-click the program with which the file was last opened, or the folder it was located in. Note that a previous version will be available only if a backup or restore point was created prior to the file being deleted.

Menu Bars Are Missing

In versions of Windows prior to Vista and 7, all Explorer windows had a menu bar at the top providing File, Edit, View, Tools and Help options.

With Windows Vista and Windows 7, this menu bar has been removed. If you are one of the many users who would like to get this back, do the following:

1 Open any explorer window

2 Click Organize, Layout and then select Menu bar. It will now be permanently restored on all folders

If you are using Internet Explorer 8 or 9, again the menu bar will be missing in the browser. You can retrieve it in similar fashion.

1 Open Internet Explorer

2 Right-click anywhere in the blue section at the top of the window and click Menu Bar. It will now be restored

(13) Miscellaneous

In the final chapter, we look at some miscellaneous issues. These range from the merely irritating, e.g. User Account Control and Problem Reports, to more serious problems such as Windows Explorer crashing and USB3 devices not working.

Aero Snap

Aero Snap is a Windows 7 feature designed to make the manipulation of open Windows easier. For example, drag a window to the left side of the desktop and it will fill half of the screen. Drag another window to the right side of the desktop and it will fill the other half of the screen.

Also, you can move a window to the top of the desktop and it will automatically maximise. Move it down slightly and it will revert to its original size.

Many users have found the latter part of this feature to be somewhat annoying as it is very easy to maximise a window inadvertently thus hiding other windows being worked in.

It can be disabled as follows:

1 Go to Start, Control Panel, Ease of Access Center

2 Click "Make the mouse easier to use"

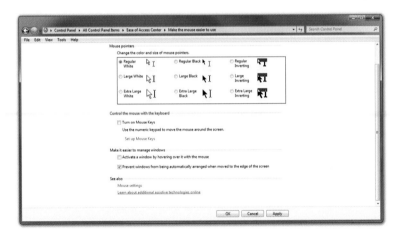

3 Check the "Prevent windows from being automatically arranged when moved to the edge of the screen" checkbox

Now you will be able to arrange your window layout without interference from Windows.

Aero Peek

Another new feature in Windows 7 is Aero Peek. This reveals the desktop when the cursor is placed over the Show desktop button.

Show desktop button

It does this by hiding any open windows and instead showing the outline of where they are. While this is pretty cool, it can be annoying when the cursor is moved accidentally to the button and thus hides the window you are working in.

So you can disable this feature by doing the following:

1 Right-click on an empty area of the Taskbar and click Properties

2 Remove the check from the "Use Aero Peek to preview the desktop" checkbox

AutoPlay

AutoPlay is one of those Windows features that attempts to be helpful by providing related options that the user may not know how to access. Whenever removable media (DVDs, external hard drive, USB flash drive, etc.) is connected to the PC, a dialog box opens offering options that Windows thinks is relevant to the content on the media.

Experienced Windows users, however, have no need for AutoPlay and find it is more of a nuisance than anything else. It can be disabled, or modified, as follows:

 Go to Start, Control Panel and open AutoPlay

To disable AutoPlay completely, uncheck "Use AutoPlay for all media and devices"

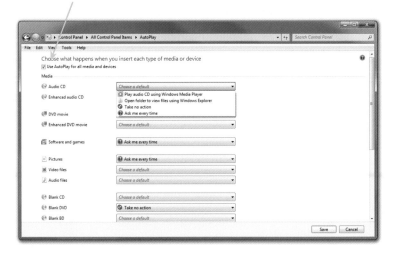

Hot tip

AutoPlay has long been regarded as an unsecure feature that provides an entry point for viruses. The version supplied with Windows 7 is much more secure.

178

However, if you find the feature useful for some media types, you can modify the way AutoPlay behaves when media of that type is connected to the PC.

For example, you can set it to automatically open your digital camera's memory card when it is connected to the PC. Just click the Pictures drop-down box and choose "Open folder to view files using Windows Explorer".

If you don't want AutoPlay to react to any other type of media, click the relevant drop-down boxes and select "Take no action".

User Account Control

User Account Control (UAC) is a security feature designed to prevent malicious software making unauthorized changes to the PC without the user's knowledge. It does this by displaying a "request permission" window when a user wants to do certain actions such as install a program, or device drivers.

It also disables the desktop (you'll see it darken when this happens as shown right). This is to prevent users being duped by spoof dialog boxes into authorizing an unsafe action.

The problem with all this though, is that these constant requests for permission quickly become tedious, especially to users who know what they are doing. If this is something you can do without, UAC can be disabled as follows:

1   Go to Start, Control Panel, User Accounts. Click "Change User Account Control Settings"

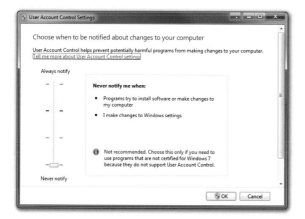

2   Drag the slider to the Never notify position

User Account Control will now be disabled. Before you do this though, be sure you are aware of the potential security ramifications – see margin note.

Hot tip

If you set UAC to never notify, i.e. off, you must be careful about which programs you run. This is because they will have the same access to the computer as you do, which includes reading and making changes to protected system areas, your personal data, and anything else stored on the computer. Programs will also be able to communicate with, and transfer information, to and from anything your computer is connected to, including the Internet.

Problem Reports

Every time an application experiences an error and is closed down by the system, Windows Problem Reporting utility will spring to life asking if you want to send details about the problem to Microsoft.

If you're the one in a million who will actually do this, then read no further. If you've no intention of complying though, you'll want to get rid of this irritation as soon as possible.

Don't forget

Before you disable Problem Reports, you should be aware that if it is available, Microsoft will send you the solution to the problem. So while it is undoubtedly irritating, it may help you to avoid a repeat occurrence of the issue.

180

1 Go to Start, Control Panel and click Administrative Tools. Then click Services

2 In the dialog box that opens, scroll down to Windows Error Reporting Service and in the drop-down box next to Startup type, select Disabled

Windows Explorer has Crashed

Occasionally, Windows Explorer, which is the application responsible for the Taskbar, Desktop and Start Menu, will crash. When this happens, the Taskbar and all the Desktop icons will disappear leaving a blank screen. With nothing to click, the user seemingly has no options with which to recover.

The solution is simple:

Don't forget

To open the Task Manager when you have no access to the Taskbar, press Ctrl+Shift+Esc.

1 Press Ctrl+Shift+Esc. This opens the Task Manager

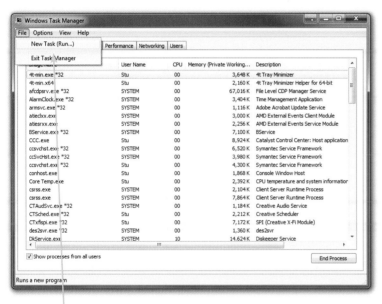

2 From the File menu, click New Task (Run...)

3 In the Open box, type explorer and then click OK

Windows will now restart Windows Explorer, which will in turn reinstate the Taskbar, Start Menu and Desktop.

A Program Won't Close

You close a program but instead of disappearing gracefully and without fuss, it insists on hanging around. You click the red X button repeatedly but it refuses to go.

When this happens, after a few moments a dialog box will open asking whether you want to wait until the program closes or to close it yourself. The latter option will usually do the trick; however, it doesn't always work.

In this situation, try the following:

1 Right-click the Taskbar and click Task Manager

Beware

If you haven't saved your data, closing a non-responding application with the Task Manager may result in you losing that data.

Hot tip

Every now and again, you will open a web page that causes your browser to stop responding. Use this procedure to close it.

2 Click the Applications tab and you will see the non-responding program. Select it and then click End Task

Hot tip

If you can't close a program even with the Task Manager then it is well and truly frozen. Your only recourse in this situation is to reboot the computer.

3 If even this doesn't work, right-click the program and click Go To Process. Then click the End Process button

Windows Update Reboots PC

Windows Update is an important feature of Windows as it enables Microsoft to keep users, PCs up-to-date. This is particularly so with regard to updates that fix security vulnerabilities in the operating system.

For this reason, the default setting for Windows Update is to automatically download and install updates. To minimize inconvenience to users it does this at 3.00am.

Many of these updates require a system reboot to complete the installation and, in the automatic mode, this is done automatically. However, this does cause problems when users have left unsaved work on the PC overnight. When they go to the PC the next day, they will find that the automatic reboot has closed their application/s and thus the unsaved work is lost.

Another common scenario is leaving a large download running overnight. The automatic reboot may terminate the download before it completes. The solution to this problem is to alter the settings of Windows Update.

1 Go to Start, Control Panel, Windows Update. On the left-hand side, click Change settings

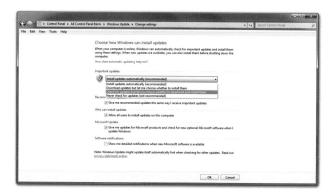

2 In the Important updates drop-down box, select "Check for updates but let me choose whether to download and install them"

With this option selected, Windows will notify users when updates are available but leave the decision of when to download and install the updates to them.

USB3 Devices Don't Work

You've bought a device that runs on the new USB3 interface but when you connect it to your PC, it doesn't work. This is almost certainly because your computer is not modern enough to support USB3. There are two solutions to this:

The first is to install Windows 7 Service Pack 1. This updates the operating system to provide USB3 support, and can be done by either manually downloading it from the Microsoft website, or using the Windows Update service to do it for you.

However, for reasons we won't go into, this is not guaranteed to work. In this case, you will have to upgrade your PC. Here, you have two options:

The first is to buy a USB3 expansion card as shown below. Install it by connecting it to a spare expansion card socket on the motherboard.

There are three things to consider when buying one of these devices: First, are you technically adept enough to open the system case and connect it to the motherboard? Second, make sure it provides enough sockets for your needs – some cards provide only one socket while others provide anything up to five. Third, make sure your PC provides the interface used by the card.

Remember, USB3 expansion cards are as new as USB3 itself, so virtually all of them use the PCI-Express interface. If your PC is several years old there is a very good chance that it uses the older PCI expansion card interface. If it does, you won't be able to connect a USB3 expansion card.

If this is the case, you will have to take the second option, which is to upgrade your motherboard.

Windows Aero Doesn't Work

Windows Aero is the graphical interface used in Windows 7 and Windows Vista. There are quite a few aspects of Aero, the more obvious of which include:

- Transparent glass effect window borders

- Taskbar thumbnails

- Window management, such as Aero Snap

- Jumplists

It is a very nice and intuitive interface but, unfortunately, many users have problems with it. If you are one of these, the following may help:

First, is Aero enabled? Right-click the desktop and click Personalize. Then select any of the Aero themes.

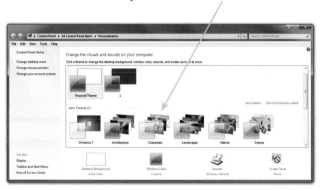

If it still doesn't work, the next thing to check is that your PC's hardware is capable of running Aero. The requirements are:

- 1 GHz, or faster, Central Processing Unit (CPU)

- 1 GB of memory

- A video system with at least 128 MB of built-in memory, plus support for DirectX 9 and Pixel Shader 2.0

In a system lacking any of the above, Aero won't work.

If Aero has stopped working after the installation of a video card, updating the PCs performance score (which automatically enables Aero) may do the trick. Do this as follows:

Hot tip

You should also make sure the video card's driver is the latest version.

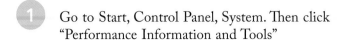

Go to Start, Control Panel, System. Then click "Performance Information and Tools"

Click Refresh Now. If your system is capable of running Aero it should now work.

In a situation where the problem is just lack of window transparency, the cause is likely to be that the PC is in power saving mode. The transparency feature uses a lot of system resources and so Windows may have switched it off to save power.

Go to Start, Control Panel, Power Options

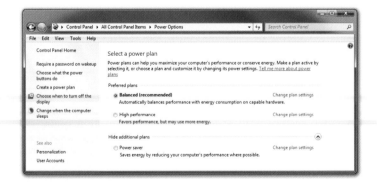

If the PC is in power saving mode, change it to "Balanced (recommended)".

Index

N

O

P

R

S

V

T

W

U